NINJA SLUSHI RECIPE BOOK FOR BEGINNERS

2000 Days of Frozen Drinks, Smoothies & Fun for the whole Family

LYDIA FROSTWELL

Published by
GRAPEVINE BOOKS

www.grapevinebooks.com
email: contact@grapevinebooks.com

Ordering Information:
Quantity sales: Special discounts are available on quantity purchases
by corporations, associations, and others.
For details, reach out to the publisher.

First published by Grapevine Books, 2025

CONTENTS

CHAPTER 1: Welcome to the World of Slushies

Slushies are more than just icy drinks. They're little frozen adventures in a cup. Whether you're cooling off on a hot summer day, throwing a party, or just craving something sweet and fruity, slushies are the perfect treat. Best of all, they're fun and easy to make at home.

So, what is a slushie? A slushie is a drink made by blending ice with flavored liquids like fruit juice, soda, syrup, or even sherbet. The result is a cold, frosty, colorful drink with a texture somewhere between a snow cone and a smoothie. Unlike a smoothie, which is often thicker and creamier, a slushie is all about the icy texture.

Slushies come in many flavors. From fruity favorites like strawberry, peach, and mango to fun combos like blue raspberry-lemonade or tropical pineapple-punch, the options are endless. You can make slushies that are sweet, sour, fizzy, creamy, or even low in sugar. Some people love adding soda or fruit punch to their slushies. Others mix in frozen berries or a swirl of sherbet for extra flavor.

One of the best parts of making slushies at home is how creative you can get. Want to layer colors? Try a rainbow slushie. Want to go low-sugar? Use fresh fruit and skip the syrup. Want to make it creamy? Blend in a scoop of yogurt or a splash of coconut milk.

And guess what? Slushies aren't just for kids. Teens and adults love them too. They're great for family nights, outdoor parties, and cooling down after a day in the sun. With a Ninja blender or slushie machine, you can whip up these fun drinks in just a few minutes.

In this book, you'll find over **2000** days' worth of slushie and smoothie recipes. There's something for everyone—whether you're a complete beginner or just looking for fresh new ideas. We'll show you how to use your blender or appliance, mix flavors like a pro, and create colorful drinks your whole family will love.

Get ready to pour, swirl, and chill. The world of slushies is wide open. And it all starts with a blender.

CHAPTER 2: Ninja Blender Basics & Appliance Care

Before we dive into recipes, it's important to know your tools. Your Ninja blender is your best friend in this frozen journey. It's powerful, quick, and perfect for crushing ice, blending fruit, and whipping up the perfect slushie texture.

Let's break it down step by step.

How to Use Your Ninja Blender for Slushies

1. *Add liquids first:* Start with juice, soda, lemonade, or water. This helps everything blend smoothly.

2. *Add fruit or flavoring next:* You can add fresh or frozen fruit, syrup, or sherbet. Frozen fruit helps keep the slushie cold.

3. *Add ice last:* Use about **1** to **2** cups of ice for most slushie recipes. Crushed ice blends better than large cubes.

4. *Blend on high:* Use the "crush," "ice," or "smoothie" setting if your blender has one. Blend for **20–30** seconds until smooth but still icy.

5. *Serve immediately:* Slushies melt quickly, so pour them right away and enjoy.

If you're using a Ninja Creami or another slushie maker, follow the specific instructions that came with the machine. These machines often require freezing the ingredients ahead of time and then spinning them into a smooth texture.

Cleaning & Caring for Your Blender

Taking care of your blender keeps it working longer and ensures your drinks always taste fresh.

- *Rinse right after use:* Don't let sticky fruit or syrup dry inside the pitcher.
- *Use warm, soapy water:* After rinsing, wash the pitcher, lid, and blades by hand or in the dishwasher (if dishwasher safe).
- *Be careful with the blades*: They're sharp. Always remove them carefully and store them safely.
- *Wipe the base with a damp cloth*: Never submerge the base in water.
- *Check the seals*: If your blender leaks, the rubber seal might be dirty or worn out. Wash it gently and check for cracks.

- *Store it properly:* Keep your blender dry, clean, and plugged out when not in use.

Tips for Blending Success

- Don't overfill the pitcher. Leave some space for the ingredients to move around.
- If the blender gets stuck, stop and stir. Add a splash of liquid to loosen it.
- Always put the lid on tightly before blending.

By mastering your Ninja blender or slushie machine, you're already halfway to slushie success. Whether you're blending berries, pouring soda, or swirling syrup, you're about to become a frozen drink expert.

Now that you've met your tools and learned the basics, it's time to dive into delicious recipes. From here on out, it's all about flavor, fun, and frozen joy.

Let's blend!

CHAPTER 3: The Science of Frozen Drinks & Smoothies

What makes a slushie a slushie and not just flavored ice? It's all about the texture and temperature. A slushie is made when tiny ice crystals are suspended in a thick, flavored liquid. You want it to be cold, smooth, and just soft enough to sip through a straw.

To get this perfect texture, the ratio of liquid to ice is important. Too much liquid, and your drink will be watery. Too much ice, and your blender might jam or give you a chunky mix. The magic happens when you find that just-right mix of cold and flavor.

Smoothies are different. They're usually made with frozen fruits, yogurt, or milk. They're thicker and creamier, and they hold their chill longer. You can still enjoy them as frozen treats, but they don't have the icy bite of a slushie.

There's also a difference in how they feel. A smoothie feels like a frozen milkshake. A slushie feels like a snow cone that melts in your mouth.

Here's something fun: the colder your drink, the sweeter it can taste. Cold temperatures dull bitterness, so frozen fruit and syrups often taste better than they do at room temperature. That's why slushies are great for combining bold flavors like lemonade, blue raspberry, or tropical fruit punch.

If you're trying to stay hydrated, slushies are a fun way to do it. Just mix water or electrolyte drinks with fruit and ice for a frosty hydration boost. And if you're aiming for healthier drinks, smoothies made with natural yogurt, frozen berries, and a splash of juice can be a perfect low-sugar treat.

Slushies aren't just science—they're art too. Layering different colors and flavors, swirling in creamy toppings, or pouring over crushed ice adds your own creative twist.

With a little know-how, your Ninja blender can become your favorite frozen science lab. Each blend is a chance to explore, experiment, and sip something amazing.

CHAPTER 4: Slushie vs Smoothie – What's the Difference?

It's easy to mix up slushies and smoothies. They're both cold, fruity, and blended in your kitchen. But they're not the same—and each one brings something special to the table.

Let's break it down.

Slushies:

- Made with crushed ice and flavored liquids like juice, soda, or syrup.
- Light and icy with a snow-cone-like texture.
- Refreshing, quick to make, and perfect for hot days.
- Great for parties, kids, and fun fruity flavors.
- Can include sherbet or soda for extra sweetness and fizz.

Slushies are perfect when you want something cold, sweet, and not too heavy. They melt faster than smoothies, so they're best enjoyed right away. You can make blue raspberry slushies for a pool party, or pour mango-lemonade slushies into colorful cups with swirly straws.

Smoothies:

- Made with frozen fruit, yogurt, milk, or juice.
- Thick, creamy, and more filling.
- Great for breakfast, snacks, or healthy treats.
- Often include bananas, berries, or tropical fruit.
- Can be low in sugar and high in nutrients.

Smoothies are ideal when you're hungry and need something energizing. A smoothie with strawberries, yogurt, and a little honey is both delicious and good for you. Teens and adults often love smoothies as post-workout or breakfast drinks.

When to Choose Each:

- Want a fun dessert or party drink? Go for a slushie.
- Want something creamy and nourishing? Try a smoothie.
- Need something cold and hydrating fast? Slushies win.
- Want to add spinach, oats, or protein? Smoothies are better.

Some recipes even blend the two. You can make a smoothie with slushie texture by using crushed ice and frozen fruit. Or you can make a slushie creamy with a swirl of sherbet or frozen yogurt.

The good news is, your Ninja blender can do both. It crushes ice for slushies and purees fruit for smoothies. You can use it to make soda slushies, strawberry smoothies, peach ice blends, and more—all in just minutes.

As you move through the recipes in this book, you'll learn how to balance ice and liquid, sweet and sour, and texture and flavor. Some drinks will be light and frosty. Others will be thick and smooth. But they'll all be delicious.No matter what you're blending, the most important thing is to have fun with it. Slushies and smoothies are more than drinks. They're cool, colorful, creative treats that bring people together.

CHAPTER 5: Essential Tools – Machine, Maker, Shaved Ice & More

You don't need fancy equipment to make a good slushie or smoothie, but having the right tools can make the process easier, faster, and way more fun. Let's take a look at what you'll need.

1. Blender (Your Ninja Hero)

A strong blender is the heart of your setup. Ninja blenders are perfect for this because they can crush ice, puree frozen fruit, and blend even thick smoothies. Look for features like "Ice Crush," "Frozen Drink," or "Smoothie" modes. If yours has presets, that's even better.

2. Slushie Maker or Machine

If you're really into slushies, you might want a dedicated slushie maker. These machines freeze and spin your drink to the perfect consistency, kind of like what you see at gas stations or snack bars. They're great for parties or big batches. Some models even let you use soda or juice directly.

3. Ice Options – Crushed vs Cubes vs Shaved

Ice matters! Regular cubes work, but crushed ice blends more easily. Shaved ice gives a snow-cone texture that's perfect for layering and pouring syrups over. If you don't have crushed or shaved ice, pulse your blender a few times before adding other ingredients.

4. Measuring Tools

Keep a few measuring cups and spoons nearby. Getting the right balance between ice, liquid, and sweeteners will help you avoid drinks that are too watery or too chunky.

5. Cups, Straws & Spoons

Serve your slushies in tall clear cups to show off the fun colors. Wide straws are great for sipping thicker drinks. Spoons come in handy for layered slushies and smoothie bowls.

6. Storage Containers & Ice Cube Trays

Want to prep ahead? Freeze fruit in small bags or trays. Make flavored ice cubes using juice or soda. Keep toppings like frozen berries or syrups ready in the fridge for quick blending.

With just a few of these items, you're ready to mix, blend, pour, and swirl your way into slushie magic. It's all about being prepared and having fun with the process.

CHAPTER 6: Stocking Your Slushie Pantry – Syrups, Fruits & Mix-ins

Let's talk ingredients! A well-stocked slushie pantry means you can create fun frozen drinks any time. Whether you love fruity, fizzy, sweet, sour, creamy, or low-sugar, there are so many ingredients to explore.

1. Liquids (Base of the Drink)

Start with one of these:

- Juices: Orange, apple, cranberry, grape, pineapple, mango.
- Sodas: Lemon-lime, cola, root beer, cream soda, fruit-flavored.
- Lemonade & Limeade: Adds tang and brightness.
- Coconut water: Light, hydrating, and tropical.
- Milk or Plant-Based Milks: For creamy smoothies.
- Iced Tea or Fruit Punch: Great for refreshing drinks.

2. Fruits (Frozen or Fresh)

Keep a mix of frozen and fresh fruits on hand. Frozen fruit doubles as ice and flavor.

- Berries: Strawberries, blueberries, raspberries.
- Tropical: Mango, pineapple, banana.
- Citrus: Orange slices, lemon zest.
- Others: Watermelon, peach, kiwi, grapes.

Pro tip: Cut and freeze ripe fruit in small chunks to use anytime.

3. Syrups & Sweeteners

Syrups bring bold flavor and fun colors. You don't need much!

- Blue raspberry, cherry, grape, cotton candy, watermelon.
- Simple syrup (sugar + water boiled and cooled).

- Maple syrup, agave, or honey for smoothies.

Try mixing syrups with soda or layering flavors for extra excitement.

4. Add-ins & Mix-ins

Customize your drinks with these extras:

- Yogurt (for creamy smoothies).
- Sherbet or sorbet (adds flavor and texture).
- Ice cream or whipped topping (dessert-style drinks).
- Fruit punch concentrate or drink powder.
- Lemon or lime juice for a tart twist.

5. Toppings & Garnishes

Take your slushie from good to amazing with:

- Colorful sprinkles.
- Mini marshmallows.
- Shaved coconut.
- Slices of fresh fruit.
- Cherries or fruit skewer toppers.

6. Low-Sugar & Healthy Options

Want to keep things light? No problem.

- Use fresh fruit and no added syrup.
- Choose low-sugar juices or unsweetened coconut water.
- Add veggies like spinach or cucumber to smoothies.
- Use Greek yogurt or nut milk for creaminess.

Your Flavor Kit at a Glance:

- **3** juices
- **2** sodas
- **4** types of fruit (fresh or frozen)
- **2** syrups
- **1** creamy element (like yogurt)

- Ice, ice, ice!

Having these staples makes it easy to mix and match ingredients. Soon, you'll be able to look at what's in your kitchen and think, "Let's turn this into a slushie!"

CHAPTER 7: Tips for Quick, Easy, Homemade Recipes

Making slushies and smoothies at home is simple, but a few small tricks can make a big difference. Whether you're in a hurry or blending for fun, these tips will help you get great results every time.

1. Use Frozen Fruit as Ice

Instead of adding too many ice cubes, use frozen fruit. It keeps the drink cold while adding flavor and nutrients. Bananas, strawberries, mangoes, and blueberries all work great.

2. Prep Ingredients in Advance

Cut and freeze fruit ahead of time in small bags. Pre-measure your favorite juice or syrup into jars. This way, when you're ready to blend, everything is just a quick pour away.

3. Keep the Blender Clean and Ready

A clean, dry blender means you're always ready to make something delicious. Rinse it after every use, and leave it on the counter so you remember to use it.

4. Use Clear Cups to Show Off Colors

Slushies look amazing in see-through cups. Layer different colors like blue raspberry and strawberry for a rainbow effect. Kids especially love colorful drinks they can see.

5. Start Small, Then Add

If you're trying a new flavor mix, start with a small amount. You can always add more syrup, fruit, or juice. It's easier to build flavor than fix a mix that's too strong.

6. Choose Your Sweetness Level

Taste as you go. Some fruits, like ripe mango or pineapple, are naturally sweet. Others, like lemon or cranberry, may need a little syrup or honey to balance them out.

7. Smooth First, Then Chill Again

If your slushie is too watery, pop it in the freezer for **10–15** minutes. Give it a quick stir, and it'll be icy again. This works well when making large batches.

8. Make It a Fun Activity

Let kids or friends pick their own ingredients. Set up a little slushie station with fruit, ice, and mix-ins. It turns drink-making into a creative party.

9. Store Leftovers for Later

Freeze any extra slushie in a popsicle mold or ice cube tray. Later, you can blend the cubes with a splash of juice for a quick icy treat.

With these tips, you'll never be far from a frosty, refreshing drink. Slushies are fast, easy, and fun—and you're now ready to make them anytime!

CHAPTER 8: How to Create Icy, Cold Perfection Every Time

Getting the right slushie texture is the key to a great frozen drink. You want it to be smooth and icy, not too watery, not too chunky. Let's go step by step.

Step 1: Choose the Right Ice

Use small or crushed ice if you can. Large cubes are harder to blend and can leave chunks. If your ice is thick, let it sit out for a few minutes before blending to soften slightly.

Step 2: Keep Everything Cold

Start with cold juice or fruit. If everything is warm, the ice melts too fast, and you end up with a thin drink. You can even chill your blender pitcher before use.

Step 3: Use the Right Ratios

Here's a simple formula to follow:

- **1** cup liquid (juice, soda, lemonade)
- **1** to **1½** cups ice
- ½ to **1** cup fruit or mix-ins

Adjust based on your blender and how thick you like your drink. If it's too thin, add more ice. If it's too thick, add more liquid.

Step 4: Blend in Bursts

Pulse your blender in short bursts. This helps crush the ice evenly and avoids over-blending. A good slushie should be icy, but still easy to sip.

Step 5: Taste and Adjust

Before pouring, take a small spoonful. If it needs more flavor, add a splash of syrup or fruit juice. If it's too strong, add a bit of crushed ice.

Step 6: Serve Immediately

Slushies melt quickly, especially in summer. Have your cups and straws ready before you blend. Pour, swirl, and serve fast for the best experience.

Bonus Tip: Layer for Color & Fun

Want a two-tone slushie? Blend two different batches separately (like blue raspberry and lemonade), then slowly pour one on top of the other. Use a spoon to create a swirled effect. It's great for parties and photos!

For Smoothies:

- Use frozen fruit instead of ice for a thicker, creamier texture.
- Add milk, yogurt, or plant-based alternatives for creaminess.
- Blend longer for smooth, drinkable consistency.

Keep It Chill:

- Use insulated cups to keep drinks icy longer.
- Chill your fruit, juice, and blender before use.
- Always blend with care—too much time and your slushie turns to soup!

By learning how to balance ice, liquid, and flavor, you're on your way to frozen drink perfection. Every blend is a chance to get creative, cool down, and enjoy something homemade.

CHAPTER 9: Creative Mixing and Swirling Techniques

Slushies are fun to drink, but they're also fun to see. One of the best things about homemade slushies is how colorful and creative you can get. Want to swirl two flavors? Make a rainbow in a glass? Turn your drink into a snow cone tower? Here's how.

1. Layering Flavors

To make layers, blend different slushie flavors one at a time. Pour the first flavor into the cup and let it sit for **30** seconds. Then slowly pour the second flavor on top. Use a spoon to help separate the layers as you pour.

Try these combos:

- Blue raspberry + lemonade (bright and bold)
- Strawberry + mango (sweet and sunny)
- Pineapple + coconut (tropical layers)

2. Swirl Effects

Want to swirl two flavors together? Use a spoon or straw to gently twist the drink right after pouring. This works best when the two colors are bold and the textures are thick.

For a sherbet swirl: blend one flavor with a scoop of sherbet, then pour in a second slushie on top and swirl it with a spoon.

3. Rainbow Cups

Make small batches of red, orange, yellow, green, blue, and purple slushies using syrup or fruit juice. Layer them from bottom to top using the spoon trick. These are party favorites!

4. Pour Over Ice

Crushed or shaved ice in a clear cup can act as a base. Pour different syrups or slushies over it and let the colors mix as they melt. This creates a snow cone effect with slushie texture.

5. Top It Off

Add sprinkles, whipped topping, a gummy candy, or fruit skewer on top. For a fun touch, use colorful straws or swirl sticks to mix while drinking.

Mixing and swirling doesn't just look good—it makes every sip a surprise. And it turns your drink into a showstopper.

CHAPTER 10: Making Low-Sugar and Healthy Hydration Options

Slushies can be just as healthy as they are fun. If you're trying to cut back on sugar or just want to make better choices, don't worry. You can still enjoy cold, tasty drinks without loading up on syrup.

1. Use Natural Sweetness

Fruits like mango, banana, pineapple, and berries are naturally sweet. Use them frozen, and you won't need to add sugar at all. The colder the drink, the sweeter it will taste.

2. Try Low-Sugar Liquids

Choose juices that say "**100%** juice" or "no added sugar." Coconut water, herbal iced tea, and citrus-infused water are great options too. They add flavor without added sweetness.

3. Go for Lighter Syrups or Skip Them

If using syrup, add just a teaspoon at a time. You can also make your own light syrup at home using fruit juice and a small amount of honey or agave. Mix and boil, then cool and store in the fridge.

4. Add Veggies to Smoothies

Spinach, kale, cucumber, or even avocado can go into smoothies without changing the taste too much. Blend with fruit and a little citrus to keep it fresh. Kids won't even notice the greens.

5. Use Ice, Not Ice Cream

For a light, icy texture, skip the creamy toppings and stick with blended ice and fruit. If you want something smooth, try using Greek yogurt instead of sherbet or cream.

6. Hydration Slushies

These are perfect for hot days or sports practice. Use:

- Coconut water or electrolyte drinks
- Frozen watermelon or orange slices

- A squeeze of lime
- Ice

Blend and enjoy a refreshing, healthy boost.

7. Portion Control

Make smaller cups or use narrow glasses to keep portion sizes balanced. Slushies are easy to sip quickly, so serving less means you enjoy it longer.

Healthy Flavor Ideas:

- Pineapple + mint
- Cucumber + lemon + ice
- Strawberry + coconut water
- Watermelon + lime
- Mango + Greek yogurt

You don't have to give up flavor to eat smart. With just a few swaps, you'll have slushies and smoothies that are refreshing, colorful, and good for your body too.

PART 1

Tea-Based Slushie Recipes

1: Peach Green Tea Slushie

Fruity, fresh, and lightly caffeinated, this slushie tastes like a summer afternoon in a cup.

You'll Need:

- **1** cup brewed green tea (chilled)
- ½ cup frozen peach slices
- Juice of ½ lemon
- Ice as needed

How to Make It:

1. Brew green tea and let it cool completely.

2. Blend with peaches, lemon juice, and ice until slushy.

3. Serve with a lemon slice or mint leaf.

Tea Tip: Use jasmine green tea for a floral twist.

It's light, fruity, and a great alternative to store-bought iced teas.

2: Hibiscus Berry Slushie

This naturally tangy tea makes a deep red slushie that's both refreshing and packed with antioxidants.

You'll Need:

- ¾ cup brewed hibiscus tea (chilled)
- ½ cup frozen raspberries or mixed berries
- ½ teaspoon lime juice
- Ice

How to Make It:

1. Brew hibiscus tea and chill.

2. Blend with berries, lime juice, and ice until icy.

3. Serve in a clear glass to show off the color.

Tart Twist: Add a few mint leaves for contrast.

It's fruity, floral, and ideal for a cooling afternoon treat.

3: Chai Spice Slushie

A cool version of a cozy classic—this chai slushie brings cinnamon, clove, and cardamom to frozen life.

You'll Need:

- ¾ cup strong brewed chai tea (chilled)
- ½ frozen banana
- ¼ cup milk or almond milk
- Ice
- Optional: sprinkle of cinnamon or nutmeg

How to Make It:

1. Brew chai and chill completely.

2. Blend with banana, milk, and ice until thick.

3. Serve with a dusting of cinnamon on top.

Creamy Twist: Add a spoon of vanilla yogurt for extra body.

Perfect for tea lovers who want the spice without the heat.

4: Lemon Ginger Tea Slushie

Zesty and sharp, this tea-based slushie is perfect when you want something cleansing and cold.

You'll Need:

- ¾ cup brewed lemon ginger tea (chilled)
- Juice of ½ lemon
- ½ teaspoon grated ginger (optional)
- Ice
- Optional: touch of stevia or monk fruit

How to Make It:

1. Brew tea and cool it.

2. Blend with lemon juice, ginger, and ice until icy.

3. Sweeten to taste if needed.

Wellness Tip: This one's perfect for digestion or post-meal refreshment.

It's sharp, clean, and naturally invigorating.

5: Matcha Mango Slushi

A modern green tea slushie that blends matcha's calm energy with tropical mango flavor.

You'll Need:

- ½ teaspoon matcha powder
- ¾ cup water or almond milk
- ½ cup frozen mango chunks
- Ice
- Optional: honey or maple syrup to taste

How to Make It:

1. Whisk matcha into water or milk.
2. Blend with mango and ice until thick.
3. Serve with a sprinkle of matcha on top.

Flavor Tip: Add a squeeze of lime for brightness.

It's rich in antioxidants, vibrant in flavor, and great for focus.

PART 2: Sugar-Free Slushie Recipes

6: Cucumber Mint Lime Slushie

Clean, crisp, and hydrating—this sugar-free slushie is packed with fresh flavor and perfect for hot days.

You'll Need:

- ½ cucumber, peeled and chopped
- Juice of **1** lime
- A few fresh mint leaves
- ¾ cup cold water or coconut water
- **1** cup crushed ice

How to Make It:

1. Blend cucumber, lime juice, mint, and water with ice.
2. Pour into a chilled glass and garnish with extra mint.

Cool Tip: Add a pinch of sea salt for an electrolyte boost.

This drink is bright, naturally sugar-free, and spa-refreshing.

7: Strawberry Basil Slushie

Sweet berries and fragrant basil combine in this sophisticated yet simple slushie.

You'll Need:

- **1** cup frozen strawberries
- **3–4** fresh basil leaves
- Juice of ½ lemon
- ¾ cup cold water
- Ice if needed

How to Make It:

1. Blend strawberries, basil, lemon juice, and water until slushy.
2. Pour and serve with a basil leaf on top.

Natural Sweetness: Ripe strawberries bring enough flavor—no need for added sugar.

It's refreshing, fruity, and surprisingly elegant.

8: Pineapple Ginger Chill

Tropical pineapple gets a spicy zing from ginger in this sugar-free slushie with a kick.

You'll Need:

- **1** cup frozen pineapple chunks
- ½ teaspoon fresh grated ginger
- Juice of ½ lime
- ¾ cup coconut water
- Ice as needed

How to Make It:

1. Blend pineapple, ginger, lime, and coconut water until smooth.
2. Pour and serve with a slice of lime or pineapple.

Spicy Option: Add more ginger for extra heat.

This slushie is immune-boosting, vibrant, and perfect for mornings.

9: Blackberry Lemonade Slushie

Tart blackberries and fresh lemon combine for a sugar-free spin on frozen lemonade.

You'll Need:

- **1** cup frozen blackberries
- Juice of **1** lemon
- ¾ cup cold water
- Ice
- Optional: stevia or monk fruit to taste

How to Make It:

1. Blend blackberries, lemon juice, and water with ice.
2. Taste and sweeten naturally if desired.
3. Pour into a clear cup and garnish with a lemon wheel.

Berry Tip: Strain after blending if you prefer a smoother texture.

It's tangy, bold, and refreshingly tart—great for sipping outside.

10: Apple Cinnamon Slushie

This cozy-meets-cold drink is sweetened only by apple, with warm cinnamon flavor and no sugar at all.

You'll Need:

- **1** large apple (peeled and chopped)
- ½ frozen banana
- ½ teaspoon ground cinnamon
- ¾ cup water or brewed herbal tea
- Ice

How to Make It:

1. Blend apple, banana, cinnamon, and water with ice until slushy.

2. Pour and dust the top with a little extra cinnamon.

Comforting Twist: Use chilled chamomile tea instead of water for an added calming effect.

This drink tastes like a chilled apple pie—naturally sweet and sugar-free.

PART 3: Fruity & Fun Favorites

11: Classic Strawberry Slushie

This bright pink treat is a classic for a reason—sweet, juicy, and bursting with flavor. It's an easy go-to when you want something fruity and refreshing.

You'll Need:

- **1** cup frozen strawberries
- ¾ cup lemonade or cold water
- **1** cup ice
- **1** tablespoon honey or simple syrup (optional)
- ½ teaspoon lemon juice

How to Make It:

1. Add lemonade, frozen strawberries, and ice to the blender.
2. Drizzle in honey if desired.
3. Blend until smooth and icy.
4. Pour into a clear glass and serve with a wide straw.

Fun Twist: Use strawberry soda instead of lemonade for a fizzy version.

12: Mango Magic Smoothie

This smoothie tastes like sunshine. It's creamy, sweet, and a favorite among kids and adults alike.

You'll Need:

- **1** cup frozen mango chunks
- ½ banana
- ¾ cup orange or mango juice
- ¼ cup vanilla yogurt
- **1** teaspoon honey (optional)

How to Make It:

1. Blend juice, mango, banana, and yogurt.
2. Add honey if your fruit isn't sweet enough.
3. Blend until thick and creamy.
4. Serve cold with a sprinkle of cinnamon or shredded coconut.

Tip: Add a splash of coconut milk to make it a tropical dream.

13: Peach Party Chill

This peachy slushie is perfect for summer. It's icy, light, and great for a backyard party.

You'll Need:

- **1** cup frozen peach slices
- ¾ cup peach juice or white grape juice
- **1** cup ice
- **1** teaspoon lemon juice
- Optional: fresh peach slice for garnish

How to Make It:

1. Blend juice, peaches, lemon juice, and ice until slushy.
2. Pour into a chilled glass.
3. Garnish with a peach slice.

Party Tip: Make a big batch in a pitcher and serve with rainbow straws for guests.

14: Pineapple Paradise Punch

Tart, sweet, and tropically refreshing. This drink brings beach vibes no matter where you are.

You'll Need:

- **1** cup frozen pineapple
- ½ banana (for creaminess)
- ¾ cup pineapple juice
- ½ cup coconut water
- **1** teaspoon agave or honey (optional)

How to Make It:

1. Add juice, pineapple, banana, and coconut water to blender.
2. Blend until smooth and frosty.

3. Taste and sweeten if needed.

4. Pour into a glass and top with shredded coconut.

Fun Idea: Serve with a paper umbrella or tropical fruit skewer.

15: Blue Raspberry Freeze

Bright blue, icy cold, and packed with fun flavor. This slushie is great for kids, parties, and colorful drink lovers.

You'll Need:

- **1** cup crushed ice
- ¾ cup cold water or lemon-lime soda
- **2** tablespoons blue raspberry syrup
- Optional: lemon slice or candy topper

How to Make It:

1. Pour liquid and syrup into blender.
2. Add crushed ice.
3. Blend until icy and bright blue.
4. Pour and enjoy with a twisty straw.

Cool Tip: Mix with strawberry slush for a red-and-blue swirl.

16: Citrus Explosion – Orange, Lemon, Lime

Zingy, tangy, and full of citrus sparkle. This slushie is super refreshing and perfect for hot days.

You'll Need:

- Juice of **1** orange, **1** lemon, and **1** lime
- **1** cup crushed ice
- **1** tablespoon honey or agave
- ½ cup water or sparkling water

How to Make It:

1. Squeeze your citrus fruits and strain out the seeds.
2. Blend the juice with water, ice, and sweetener.
3. Pour and serve immediately.

Bonus Option: Freeze orange slices and blend those in too.

17: Tropical Breeze Smoothie

This smoothie is a creamy blend of tropical fruits that feels like a vacation in a glass.

You'll Need:

- ½ cup frozen pineapple
- ½ cup frozen mango
- ¼ banana
- ½ cup orange juice
- ¼ cup Greek yogurt or coconut milk
- Optional: chia seeds or shredded coconut

How to Make It:

1. Combine all ingredients in the blender.
2. Blend until thick and creamy.
3. Pour into a tall glass and top with coconut flakes.

Healthy Tip: Add spinach for a green twist with no strong veggie taste.

18: Fruit Punch Fizz

This slushie is a bold mix of juicy fruit flavors and fizzy fun. It's the perfect party drink—colorful, sweet, and always a hit with kids and teens.

You'll Need:

- ¾ cup fruit punch
- ½ cup lemon-lime soda
- **1** cup crushed ice
- ½ cup frozen mixed fruit (like mango, pineapple, or berries)
- Optional: maraschino cherry on top

How to Make It:

1. Add fruit punch and soda to the blender.
2. Toss in the ice and frozen fruit.
3. Blend until icy and smooth.
4. Pour into a fun glass and top with a cherry or slice of orange.

Fizz Tip: For extra bubbles, stir in more soda after blending.

This one's like a fruit explosion with a soda sparkle. Bright, fun, and bursting with flavor!

19: Sweet Berry Blast

Berry lovers, this one's for you. Packed with strawberries, blueberries, and raspberries, this smoothie is rich in flavor and full of natural color.

You'll Need:

- ½ cup frozen strawberries
- ¼ cup frozen blueberries
- ¼ cup frozen raspberries
- ¾ cup apple or grape juice
- **1** teaspoon honey (optional)
- **1** tablespoon Greek yogurt (optional for creaminess)

How to Make It:

1. Add juice to the blender first.
2. Add frozen berries, honey, and yogurt.
3. Blend until smooth and thick.
4. Pour and enjoy cold.

Berry Boost: Add a spoonful of chia seeds for fiber and texture.

It's sweet, icy, and just the right amount of tart. This smoothie makes a great breakfast, snack, or colorful drink for guests.

20: Sherbet Surprise Slush

This dessert-style slushie is full of creamy, fruity fun. Choose your favorite sherbet flavor, blend it with ice and juice, and enjoy a smooth, swirly treat.

You'll Need:

- **2** scoops orange or rainbow sherbet
- ½ cup pineapple or orange juice
- **1** cup crushed ice
- Optional: splash of soda or seltzer

How to Make It:

1. Add sherbet, juice, and ice to the blender.
2. Blend until thick and creamy.
3. Add a splash of soda if you want a fizzy twist.
4. Serve with a spoon or thick straw.

Fun Tip: Try layering orange sherbet with lime slush for a citrus swirl.

This one's like a frozen dessert and drink all in one. It's colorful, creamy, and totally fun for kids and grownups.

21: Creamy Banana Smoothie

Simple and satisfying, this smoothie is a great base for mix-ins or a perfect drink on its own. It's creamy, sweet, and a favorite for breakfast.

You'll Need:

- **1** ripe banana (fresh or frozen)
- ½ cup milk or almond milk
- ¼ cup yogurt
- **1** teaspoon honey or maple syrup
- **4–5** ice cubes

How to Make It:

1. Add banana, milk, yogurt, and honey to blender.
2. Blend with ice until creamy.

3. Serve cold with a dash of cinnamon or cocoa powder.

Make It Yours: Add peanut butter or a few strawberries for extra flavor.

This smoothie is a creamy, comforting treat that's packed with natural sweetness.

22: Raspberry-Lemon Swirl

This slushie is bright, zesty, and perfect for summer. Tart lemon mixes with sweet raspberry for a cool and refreshing twist.

You'll Need:

- ½ cup frozen raspberries
- ¾ cup lemonade
- 1 cup crushed ice
- 1 tablespoon simple syrup (optional)

How to Make It:

1. Blend lemonade, raspberries, and ice until smooth.
2. Add syrup if needed for sweetness.
3. Swirl into a glass and garnish with a lemon slice.

Layer Tip: Make a second batch with just lemonade and ice to create a two-tone swirl.

It's tangy, icy, and perfect for hot afternoons. Great for grownups and kids who love bold, citrusy flavors.

23: Summer Peach & Strawberry Combo

This slushie brings together two of the best summer fruits. The blend is juicy, colorful, and just the right mix of sweet and smooth.

You'll Need:

- ½ cup frozen peach slices
- ½ cup frozen strawberries
- ¾ cup white grape juice or lemonade
- 1 cup crushed ice
- 1 teaspoon honey (optional)

How to Make It:

1. Add juice, fruit, and ice to blender.
2. Blend until slushy.
3. Taste and sweeten if needed.
4. Pour into tall glasses and top with a fruit slice.

Bonus Idea: Freeze leftovers into slushie pops.

This combo tastes like summer in a cup—bright, juicy, and refreshing.

24: Pineapple-Coconut Cream Chill

This creamy tropical smoothie feels like a mini beach vacation. Pineapple adds tang, coconut gives smoothness, and the chill factor is off the charts.

You'll Need:

- ¾ cup frozen pineapple
- ½ cup coconut milk or coconut yogurt
- ½ banana
- 1 teaspoon maple syrup (optional)
- Ice cubes for thickness

How to Make It:

1. Blend all ingredients until creamy and thick.
2. Add more ice for a frostier texture.
3. Serve in a chilled glass and top with toasted coconut.

Optional Add-in: A splash of vanilla extract for a dessert twist.

Perfect for tropical lovers, this one is creamy, rich, and naturally sweet.

25: Juicy Watermelon Splash

Light, hydrating, and bursting with fresh watermelon flavor, this slushie is a must-make for hot summer days.

You'll Need:

- **1½** cups seedless watermelon (cubed and frozen)
- **1** tablespoon lime juice
- ½ cup cold water or coconut water
- **1** teaspoon honey (optional)
- **4–5** ice cubes

How to Make It:

1. Blend frozen watermelon, lime juice, and water.
2. Add ice and blend again for a frosty finish.
3. Taste and sweeten if needed.
4. Serve with a small wedge of lime on the rim.

Hydration Hack: Mix with a splash of electrolyte drink for a cooling boost.

This slushie is light, juicy, and super refreshing—the ultimate summer cooler!

PART 4: Frozen Drinks for Every Mood

26: Slushy Snow Cone Ideas for Kids

Snow cones are simple and colorful—and kids love them. But instead of just pouring syrup over crushed ice, let's make it a real slushie-style snow cone party.

You'll Need:

- 2 cups finely crushed or shaved ice
- ½ cup fruit-flavored syrups (blue raspberry, cherry, grape, etc.)
- Colorful paper cones or cups
- Small spoons and straws

How to Make It:

1. Blend or crush ice until very fine.
2. Scoop into cones or small cups, shaping into a mound.
3. Drizzle different syrups over the top.
4. Mix colors for a rainbow look or create stripes.

Fun Ideas:

- Add gummy bears or candy sprinkles on top.
- Use frozen fruit purée instead of syrup for a healthier twist.

Snow cones are great for birthday parties, summer cookouts, or anytime you want a colorful treat that keeps kids cool and happy.

27: Frosty Party Pitchers for Teens

Teen hangouts call for big-batch, fun, and flavorful slushies. These pitcher-style recipes are perfect for movie nights, sleepovers, or casual gatherings.

You'll Need:

- 2 cups frozen strawberries
- 1½ cups orange juice
- 1 cup lemon-lime soda
- 2 cups crushed ice

How to Make It:

1. Add everything to a high-powered blender.
2. Blend until slushy and frothy.
3. Pour into a large pitcher.
4. Serve in clear cups with fresh fruit slices.

Other Pitcher Flavor Ideas:

- Tropical Punch (pineapple, mango, banana, and coconut water)
- Fizzy Peach Blend (peach juice, frozen peaches, and ginger ale)

Let teens get creative by mixing in syrups or swapping out the fruit combinations. It's slushie freedom in a pitcher!

28: Creative Lemonade Mixes

Lemonade is a perfect base for refreshing slushies. Tangy, sweet, and versatile, it blends well with fruits, herbs, or even veggies.

You'll Need:

- 1 cup homemade or store-bought lemonade
- ½ cup frozen fruit (berries, peaches, mango, etc.)
- 1 cup crushed ice
- Optional: mint, basil, or cucumber slices

How to Make It:

1. Combine lemonade, fruit, and ice in blender.
2. Blend until frosty.
3. Garnish with a lemon wheel or fresh herb.

Flavor Combos to Try:

- Blackberry-Mint Lemonade Slush
- Peach-Basil Lemonade Smoothie
- Cucumber-Lime Lemonade Chill

These drinks are hydrating, colorful, and totally customizable.

29: Soda & Syrup Combos

For a fizzy twist, try mixing soda with flavored syrups and ice. The result? Bubbly slushies that are sweet, tangy, and fun to sip.

You'll Need:

- ¾ cup chilled soda (cola, root beer, lemon-lime, or orange)
- **1–2** tablespoons flavored syrup (cherry, vanilla, blue raspberry, etc.)
- **1** cup crushed ice

How to Make It:

1. Pour soda and syrup into blender.
2. Add ice and blend until slushy.
3. Serve immediately with a colorful straw.

Tasty Combos:

- Cola + Cherry Syrup = Cherry Cola Slush
- Orange Soda + Vanilla Syrup = Creamsicle Slush
- Root Beer + Chocolate Syrup = Float-Inspired Slush

This is a great way to make dessert drinks that feel like a sweet treat without the need for ice cream.

30: Rainbow Layered Slushie

This is one of the most eye-catching slushies you'll ever make. Each layer is a different flavor and color, and when stacked carefully, it looks just like a rainbow.

You'll Need:

- A variety of fruit juices and flavored syrups in different colors
- Crushed ice
- Blender
- Clear glasses

How to Make It:

1. Blend each layer separately:
   - Red: strawberry or cherry
   - Orange: orange juice + mango
   - Yellow: lemonade
   - Green: lime or kiwi + lemon-lime soda
   - Blue: blue raspberry
   - Purple: grape juice
2. After blending, pour the first layer into a glass.
3. Freeze for **10** minutes between layers to keep colors sharp.
4. Repeat until all layers are stacked.

Tips:

- Use a spoon to gently pour each layer over the previous one.
- Let kids choose their own color order.

This drink isn't just tasty—it's also an activity!

31: Iced Coffee Smoothie

For grownups and older teens, this slushie-smoothie combo gives a caffeine boost with a creamy twist. It's great for mornings, midday pick-me-ups, or as a sweet iced treat.

You'll Need:

- **1** cup chilled brewed coffee
- ½ frozen banana
- ¼ cup milk or almond milk
- **1–2** teaspoons cocoa powder or chocolate syrup
- **1** cup ice

How to Make It:

1. Blend coffee, banana, milk, cocoa, and ice.
2. Blend until thick and creamy.
3. Pour into a glass and dust with cinnamon

or cocoa.

Make It Sweeter: Add a splash of maple syrup or vanilla extract.

This smoothie is rich, cold, and gives you energy without being heavy. Perfect for creative mornings or slow afternoons.

32: Green Power Smoothie (Spinach + Citrus)

Want something nutritious, hydrating, and still delicious? This green smoothie is packed with vitamins and flavor.

You'll Need:

- **1** cup spinach (fresh or frozen)
- ½ cup frozen pineapple
- ½ banana
- Juice of **1** orange
- ½ cup cold water or coconut water
- Ice cubes

How to Make It:

1. Blend everything until smooth and icy.
2. Add more water if it's too thick.
3. Serve with an orange wedge on the rim.

Boost It: Add chia seeds or a spoonful of yogurt for extra power.

It's green, but it tastes like fruit. Even kids who don't like spinach will love this citrus-packed smoothie.

33: Slushie Sundaes with Whipped Topping

Think slushie meets ice cream sundae. This is a layered dessert drink with sweet flavors, fun toppings, and whipped cream piled high.

You'll Need:

- **1** cup crushed ice
- ¾ cup fruit soda (strawberry, orange, or grape)
- **2** tablespoons flavored syrup
- Whipped topping
- Sprinkles, crushed cookies, or mini marshmallows

How to Make It:

1. Blend ice, soda, and syrup into a thick slush.
2. Pour into a sundae cup.
3. Add a generous swirl of whipped cream.
4. Top with sprinkles, candy, or cookies.

Fun Add-ons:

- Drizzle with chocolate syrup.
- Use a cherry on top just like a real sundae.

This drink is great for parties or rewards. It's colorful, festive, and feels like a frozen dessert in a cup.

34: Frozen Yogurt Smoothie Bowls

Smoothie bowls are thicker than regular smoothies and eaten with a spoon. Frozen yogurt gives them a creamy base, and you can top them with fruits, seeds, and crunchies for a full snack or light meal.

You'll Need:

- ½ cup frozen mixed berries
- ½ banana
- ½ cup plain or vanilla frozen yogurt
- ¼ cup milk or fruit juice
- Optional toppings: granola, shredded coconut, fresh fruit, chia seeds

How to Make It:

1. Blend berries, banana, frozen yogurt, and liquid until thick.
2. Spoon into a bowl.
3. Decorate with toppings of your choice.
4. Serve cold and eat with a spoon.

Flavor Tip: Swap berries for mango or peach for a tropical version.

This is a fun, healthy treat that feels like dessert and looks beautiful in a bowl. Great for breakfasts or cool-down snacks.

35: Cold Brew Berry Fusion

This drink is for the iced coffee lovers who also enjoy fruity blends. Cold brew coffee meets sweet berries in a bold, unique smoothie-slushie combo.

You'll Need:

- ¾ cup cold brew coffee
- ½ cup frozen strawberries or raspberries
- ½ banana
- ¼ cup milk or almond milk
- 1 teaspoon maple syrup (optional)
- Ice for texture

How to Make It:

1. Blend cold brew, berries, banana, and milk.
2. Add ice and blend again until slushy.
3. Pour into a tall glass.
4. Garnish with a fresh berry or mint leaf.

Variation: Use chocolate almond milk for a mocha-berry fusion.

This cold, fruity-coffee blend is great for mornings when you want both caffeine and a smoothie. It's creamy, icy, and packed with flavor.

36: Coconut-Pineapple Smoothie

This smoothie is rich, refreshing, and tastes like a tropical getaway. It's creamy from the coconut and sweet from the pineapple.

You'll Need:

- 1 cup frozen pineapple
- ½ banana
- ½ cup coconut milk or coconut yogurt
- ¼ cup orange juice
- Optional: honey or shredded coconut for topping

How to Make It:

1. Blend pineapple, banana, coconut milk, and juice until smooth.
2. Adjust thickness with more juice or ice.
3. Serve cold in a glass or bowl.
4. Sprinkle shredded coconut on top.

Tropical Upgrade: Add a splash of lime juice or mint for a refreshing kick.

Perfect for summer mornings or post-beach snacks, this smoothie is smooth, sweet, and hydrating.

37: Dessert-Inspired: Chocolate-Strawberry Swirl

If you love dessert but want a frozen drink version, this chocolate-strawberry swirl slushie is for you. It's rich, fruity, and fun to layer.

You'll Need:

Strawberry Layer:

- ½ cup frozen strawberries
- ½ cup lemonade
- 1 teaspoon honey

Chocolate Layer:

- ½ banana
- ½ cup milk
- 1 tablespoon cocoa powder or chocolate syrup
- 1 teaspoon vanilla extract

How to Make It:

1. Blend strawberry ingredients into a thick slush. Set aside.
2. Blend chocolate ingredients until smooth.
3. In a clear glass, alternate scoops of each mixture.

4. Use a spoon to gently swirl the layers together.

Optional Toppings: Whipped cream, chocolate shavings, or a strawberry on top.

This sweet drink looks fancy and tastes like a frozen chocolate-covered strawberry.

38: Creamy Orange Dream

This one tastes like a classic orange creamsicle, blending bright citrus and smooth vanilla. It's a nostalgic treat for adults and a dreamy drink for kids.

You'll Need:

- ¾ cup orange juice
- ¼ cup vanilla yogurt or vanilla ice cream
- ½ frozen banana
- **1** cup ice
- ½ teaspoon vanilla extract

How to Make It:

1. Blend orange juice, banana, yogurt, and vanilla.
2. Add ice and blend until creamy and frosty.
3. Pour into a chilled glass.
4. Garnish with an orange slice or whipped topping.

Fun Variation: Add a splash of cream soda for a fizzy creamsicle float.

It's sweet, creamy, and just the right amount of tart. A perfect after-dinner treat or afternoon refresher.

39: Slushie Float with Soda and Ice Cream

This drink is like a root beer float but with endless flavor combinations. Soda, syrup, and a scoop of ice cream make it fizzy, creamy, and incredibly fun.

You'll Need:

- ¾ cup cold soda (root beer, cola, orange, or lemon-lime)
- **1–2** tablespoons flavored syrup (cherry, vanilla, blue raspberry)
- **1** cup crushed ice
- **1** scoop vanilla ice cream

How to Make It:

1. Blend soda, syrup, and ice into a thick slush.
2. Pour into a tall glass.
3. Top with a scoop of vanilla ice cream.
4. Serve with a spoon and straw.

Flavor Combos to Try:

- Orange soda + vanilla = Creamsicle Float
- Cola + cherry syrup = Cherry Cola Float
- Lemon-lime soda + raspberry syrup = Fizzy Berry Float

This one's part drink, part dessert. Great for summer parties or as a fun end-of-week treat.

40: Snow Cone Mocktail Bar

Want a fun, fancy drink station for kids and adults alike? A snow cone mocktail bar lets everyone mix their own frozen drink with unique flavors, syrups, and toppings.

What **You'll Need:**

- Large batch of crushed or shaved ice
- A variety of mocktail-style syrups:
  - Strawberry-lime
  - Pineapple-mint
  - Blueberry-basil
  - Mango-ginger
- Mix-ins: soda water, lemonade, iced tea
- Toppings: fresh fruit, herbs, colorful sugar crystals

How to Set It Up:

1. Set out clear cups and spoons.

2. Offer a few base liquids like lemonade or soda.

3. Let guests fill their cups with ice.

4. Provide syrups and toppings for custom creations.

5. Use small signs to label flavor ideas.

Mocktail Combos to Try:

- "Berry Mojito" – blueberry syrup + soda water + mint

- "Tropical Fizz" – mango syrup + pineapple juice + lime

- "Sunset Splash" – strawberry syrup + lemonade + orange slice

This is perfect for birthday parties, sleepovers, or family BBQs. Everyone gets to be their own frozen drink artist!

PART 5: Family Fun & Theme Recipes

41: Birthday Bash Slushie Station

Turn any birthday into a frozen celebration with a DIY slushie station. Kids (and grownups) love mixing and matching their own icy drinks, and it's easy to set up.

What You'll Need:

- Ninja blender or slushie machine
- Prepped frozen fruits (strawberries, mangoes, pineapples)
- A few flavored syrups (blue raspberry, cherry, grape)
- Juices, soda, or lemonade as base liquids
- Ice
- Clear plastic cups, colorful straws, and toppings like whipped cream, sprinkles, and gummy candies

How to Set Up:

1. Set out the ingredients in labeled bowls.
2. Provide a simple mix chart (e.g. "Tropical = mango + pineapple + coconut water").
3. Let kids choose their base, fruit, syrup, and extras.
4. Blend, pour, and let them top their drinks.
5. Use paper umbrellas or cute labels to decorate.

This setup becomes an activity and a treat in one. It's a hands-on, customizable slushie party!

42: DIY Summer Treat Cart

Make your own summer treat cart at home for family weekends or neighborhood fun. A rolling cart or table with wheels can turn your kitchen into a frozen drink stand.

Stock Your Cart With:

- Crushed ice and pre-frozen fruit in small bags
- Juices, lemonade, and flavored soda
- Syrups, yogurt, sherbet, and whipped topping
- Cups, napkins, spoons, and cute signs

How It Works:

1. Pick a theme—like "Tropical Freeze" or "Rainbow Refresher."
2. Let each family member "order" their drink.
3. One person blends, another tops, and someone else serves.

This brings food truck fun into your kitchen or backyard. Rotate who's in charge of the cart to keep it exciting every week.

43: Kid-Friendly Blue Raspberry & Cotton Candy

This bright blue drink is a sweet, colorful treat that kids love. It's sweet, icy, and tastes just like the fair!

You'll Need:

- ¾ cup lemonade or lemon-lime soda
- **1–2** tablespoons blue raspberry syrup
- **1** cup crushed ice
- Cotton candy for garnish (optional but fun!)

How to Make It:

1. Blend soda, syrup, and ice until smooth and slushy.
2. Pour into a clear glass or cup.
3. Top with a small tuft of cotton candy just before serving.
4. Serve with a bright-colored straw.

Bonus Fun: Let kids choose a second syrup to swirl in for extra color.

This is perfect for playdates or weekend rewards and adds a wow-factor to any frozen treat.

44: Fruity Fun for Family Game Nights

Game nights get even better with a round of homemade slushies. Pick a theme, blend up a big batch, and let everyone enjoy fruity, colorful drinks between turns.

Try This Recipe:

- **1** cup frozen mixed berries
- ½ banana
- ¾ cup apple juice
- **1** cup crushed ice
- Dash of lemon or lime juice for zest

How to Make It:

1. Blend all ingredients until icy and thick.
2. Pour into small glasses with game-themed labels.
3. Offer bonus toppings like sour candy or whipped cream.

Game Night Twist: Let the winner choose the next flavor for the next round!

This turns a regular family activity into a sweet celebration everyone looks forward to.

45: Sleepover Smoothie Specials

Sleepovers call for fun snacks and frozen drinks. Make smoothies that feel like dessert but are full of fruity goodness.

Sleepover Smoothie Base:

- ½ cup frozen strawberries
- ½ cup vanilla yogurt
- ¼ banana
- ¾ cup milk or juice
- Ice

Toppings:

- Mini marshmallows
- Chocolate chips
- Whipped cream
- Crushed graham crackers

How to Make It:

1. Blend smoothie ingredients until creamy.
2. Pour into jars or cups.
3. Let each person add their favorite toppings.
4. Sip while watching a movie or playing games.

You can also create a "midnight menu" where each smoothie gets a fun name like "Pillow Punch" or "Dreamy Delight."

46: Outdoor BBQ Slushie Coolers

When the grill is on and the sun is out, nothing beats a cold slushie in hand. These frozen coolers are great for outdoor meals and pair perfectly with grilled food.

BBQ Cooler Idea:

- ½ cup frozen pineapple
- ½ cup frozen mango
- **1** cup coconut water or lemonade
- **1** cup ice
- Optional: mint or cucumber slice

How to Make It:

1. Blend everything until frosty.
2. Pour into wide-mouthed cups.
3. Serve with a skewer of fresh fruit on the rim.

Serving Tip: Make a non-alcoholic adult version by adding a splash of ginger beer or unsweetened iced tea.

Everyone from kids to grandparents will enjoy sipping these in the sunshine.

47: Frozen Drink Party Hacks

Want to level up your frozen drink game for any event? These smart hacks will keep things smooth, fast, and fun.

1. Pre-freeze Ingredients:

Freeze fruit in individual servings with juice in silicone trays. Just pop one out and blend.

2. Make a Slushie Bar Sign:

List flavor combos like "Tropical Twist = mango + pineapple + coconut water" or "Fizzy Berry = soda + berries + syrup."

3. Chill Your Cups:

Put plastic cups in the freezer **10** minutes before serving to help keep drinks icy longer.

4. Use Frozen Juice Cubes:

Freeze apple, grape, or orange juice in cubes and use them instead of regular ice for richer flavor.

5. Offer "Add-On Toppings" Stations:

Have little bowls of sprinkles, chopped fruit, gummy candies, and crushed cookies ready for guests to dress up their drinks.

6. Use Big Pitchers or Dispensers:

Make slushie base blends in bulk and let people serve themselves. Keep extra ice in a cooler nearby.

7. Label Cups with Names or Stickers:

This helps avoid confusion, especially at kids' parties or large family gatherings.

With these tips, any gathering becomes a frozen drink success—less stress, more chill, and loads of fun!

48: Citrus Spritzers for Adults

Looking for something crisp, fizzy, and a little more grown-up? Citrus spritzers are refreshing slushie-style drinks that use tart fruit and sparkling mixers for a clean, bright flavor.

You'll Need:

- ½ cup fresh grapefruit or blood orange juice
- ½ cup sparkling water or lemon-lime soda
- Juice of ½ lime
- **1** cup crushed ice
- Optional: orange or lemon slice for garnish

How to Make It:

1. Blend the citrus juices and ice until slushy.
2. Pour into a chilled glass.
3. Top off with sparkling water or soda.
4. Stir gently and garnish with a citrus slice.

Flavor Tip: Add a pinch of sea salt for a unique twist—it enhances the fruitiness.

Perfect for brunches, garden parties, or relaxing afternoons, this spritzer is light, hydrating, and has just the right amount of zing.

49: Hydration Boost Smoothies

Need a cool drink that hydrates and tastes amazing? These smoothies are packed with water-rich fruits and light ingredients that fuel your body while keeping you cool.

You'll Need:

- ½ cup frozen watermelon
- ½ cucumber (peeled and sliced)
- ½ cup coconut water
- Juice of ½ lemon
- Ice cubes

How to Make It:

1. Blend all ingredients until smooth and cold.
2. Add more ice for extra frostiness.
3. Serve with a mint leaf or cucumber slice.

Hydration Add-Ons:

- Chia seeds (soaked) for electrolytes
- A pinch of Himalayan salt for mineral balance

These smoothies are perfect post-exercise or during hot summer afternoons when you want something light, healthy, and recharging.

50: Easy Peach Lemonade Slush

This one is simple, sweet, and hits all the right notes—juicy peaches paired with tart lemonade and crushed ice for an instant summer treat.

You'll Need:

- **1** cup frozen peach slices
- ¾ cup lemonade
- **1** cup crushed ice
- **1** teaspoon honey (optional)

How to Make It:

1. Blend peaches, lemonade, and ice until slushy.
2. Taste and adjust sweetness if needed.
3. Pour into a tall glass and garnish with a peach slice or lemon twist.

Flavor Tip: Use sparkling lemonade for a fizzy twist or toss in a few mint leaves while blending.

This is one of the easiest recipes in the book—and it's always a hit with both kids and adults.

51: Mango Madness for Movie Night

Movie night calls for something cold, fruity, and fun. This mango smoothie is creamy and sweet with just the right amount of thickness to sip slowly as the movie plays.

You'll Need:

- **1** cup frozen mango chunks
- ½ banana
- ¼ cup vanilla yogurt
- ½ cup orange juice
- Ice to thicken
- Optional: mini chocolate chips or a caramel drizzle

How to Make It:

1. Blend all ingredients until thick and creamy.
2. Pour into a tall, clear cup.
3. Add a straw and toppings for extra flair.

Movie Night Tip: Serve with popcorn or candy for a homemade frozen snack combo.

This one is great for kids, teens, or adults who love that tropical mango flavor in every sip.

52: Low-Sugar Frozen Fruit Shakes

Frozen drinks don't need added sugar to taste amazing. When you use ripe fruit and natural flavors, you can enjoy a sweet, icy treat that's actually good for you.

You'll Need:

- ½ cup frozen strawberries
- ½ cup frozen mango or banana
- ¾ cup unsweetened almond milk or oat milk
- Optional: **1** date or ½ teaspoon cinnamon
- Ice if needed for thicker texture

How to Make It:

1. Blend all ingredients until thick and smooth.
2. Taste and add a touch of vanilla or cinnamon if desired.
3. Pour into a glass and top with a sprinkle of chia seeds.

No Sweetener Needed: Let the fruit do the work—frozen bananas and mangoes are naturally sweet.

This is ideal for anyone watching their sugar but still craving something cool and delicious.

53: Cold & Creamy Layered Smoothie Glasses

These layered smoothie drinks look beautiful and taste even better. You can create stripes or swirls using different fruits, colors, and textures.

Layer Ideas:

- Layer **1** (pink): Strawberries + yogurt + banana
- Layer **2** (yellow): Mango + coconut milk
- Layer **3** (green): Spinach + pineapple + apple juice

How to Make It:

1. Blend each layer separately.
2. Pour the first layer into a clear glass and freeze for **5–10** minutes.
3. Gently add the next layer, and repeat.
4. Use a spoon to swirl the edges or keep clean layers for a stripe effect.

Topping Tip: Add granola, fresh fruit, or a drizzle of honey on top.

These glasses are perfect for breakfast or afternoon snacks and make smoothie time feel fancy and fun.

54: Rainbow Ice Cube Mix-ins

Want to jazz up a plain slushie or lemonade? Rainbow ice cubes are the way to go. They're fun to make, and they melt into the drink, adding color and flavor.

What **You'll Need:**

- Ice cube trays
- Colorful juices: cherry, orange, lemon, blue raspberry, grape
- Sliced berries, citrus peel, or mint for texture

How to Make It:

1. Pour a different juice into each section of the tray.
2. Add fruit bits or mint if desired.
3. Freeze completely.
4. Drop the cubes into lemon-lime soda, coconut water, or plain lemonade.

Party Tip: Let guests build their own drinks using rainbow cubes.

It's a fun way to stay hydrated while making every glass exciting and colorful.

55: Sweet 'n Tart Berry-Lime Refreshers

This drink balances sweet berries with sharp lime for a thirst-quenching slush that feels like a frozen lemonade with a twist.

You'll Need:

- ½ cup frozen raspberries or mixed berries
- Juice of **1** lime
- ¾ cup cold water or berry-flavored sparkling water
- **1** teaspoon honey or agave (optional)
- Ice

How to Make It:

1. Blend berries, lime juice, water, and ice.
2. Taste and sweeten slightly if needed.
3. Serve in a tall cup with a lime wedge or raspberry on the rim.

Refreshing Variation: Mix with watermelon or cucumber slices for extra cooling power.

This is a great drink to beat the heat, especially when you want something tangy and light without the sugar overload.

PART 6: Candy-Inspired Slushie Recipes

56: Sour Belt Slushie

A slushie that delivers the tangy rainbow flavor of sour belts with just the right kick.

You'll Need:

- ¾ cup lemonade
- **1** tablespoon sour apple syrup
- **1** tablespoon blue raspberry syrup
- **1** tablespoon strawberry syrup
- **1** cup crushed ice
- Optional: sprinkle of citric acid or lemon zest

How to Make:

Blend all ingredients until icy. Pour and garnish with a strip of sour candy.

57: Cotton Candy Cloud Slushie

This pastel-colored drink is light, sweet, and always a hit with kids.

You'll Need:

- **1** cup lemon-lime soda
- **2** tablespoons cotton candy syrup
- **1** cup crushed ice
- Cotton candy for garnish

How to Make:

Blend soda, syrup, and ice. Top with cotton candy just before serving.

58: Bubblegum Blizzard Slushie

Bright pink and full of nostalgic sweetness, this slushie tastes just like bubblegum.

You'll Need:

- ¾ cup milk or almond milk
- **2** tablespoons bubblegum syrup
- **1** cup ice
- Optional: whipped cream, pink sprinkles, or a bubblegum ball

How to Make:

Blend milk, syrup, and ice. Serve cold with fun toppings.

59: Gummy Bear Explosion

Inspired by everyone's favorite chewy candy, this slushie is a burst of fruit flavors.

You'll Need:

- ¾ cup white grape juice
- ½ cup frozen mixed fruit
- **1** tablespoon strawberry syrup
- **1** tablespoon blue raspberry syrup
- **1** cup crushed ice
- Gummy bears for topping

How to Make:

Blend all ingredients except gummies. Pour and top with gummy bear skewers or floaters.

60: Jelly Bean Juice Slushie

A colorful, fruity drink that channels the sweet variety of a jelly bean bag.

You'll Need:

- ¼ cup each: orange juice, grape juice, strawberry juice
- **1**½ cups crushed ice
- ½ teaspoon lemon juice
- Jelly beans for garnish

How to Make:

Blend juices and ice. Pour and add jelly beans to the rim or serve with a skewer.

61: Rock Candy Raspberry Fizz

Sweet and sparkly with a candy-stick stirrer—this one's a showstopper.

You'll Need:

- ¾ cup lemon-lime soda
- **2** tablespoons raspberry syrup
- **1** cup crushed ice
- **1** rock candy stick

How to Make:

Blend soda, syrup, and ice. Pour and stir with a rock candy stick.

62: Butterscotch Cream Slushie

A smooth frozen treat with warm candy-shop flavor.

You'll Need:

- ½ cup milk
- **2** tablespoons butterscotch syrup
- **1** scoop vanilla frozen yogurt
- **1** cup crushed ice

How to Make:

Blend until creamy. Serve with a drizzle of caramel or a sprinkle of butterscotch chips.

63: Lollipop Twist Slushie

Colorful, fruity, and full of fun—just like an old-fashioned swirl lollipop.

You'll Need:

- **1** tablespoon each: cherry syrup, orange syrup, grape syrup
- ¾ cup sparkling water
- **1**½ cups crushed ice
- **1** swirl lollipop for garnish

How to Make:

Blend syrups, sparkling water, and ice. Pour and serve with a lollipop sticking out of the glass.

64: Rainbow Sherbet Soda Slushie

Inspired by the colorful sweetness of rainbow sherbet, this slushie is fizzy, smooth, and fun to look at.

You'll Need:

- ½ cup lemon-lime soda
- ½ cup orange soda
- **1** scoop rainbow sherbet
- **1** cup crushed ice
- Optional: whipped cream and rainbow sprinkles

How to Make:

Blend the sodas, sherbet, and ice until frothy and smooth. Serve in a clear glass and top with whipped cream and sprinkles for extra color.

Fun Tip: Freeze a few extra scoops of sherbet into ice cube trays and use them instead of regular ice for a smoother blend.

65: Marshmallow Pop Slushie

Sweet, creamy, and a little gooey, this slushie is inspired by marshmallows and puffed rice treats. It's like dessert in a cup.

You'll Need:

- ¾ cup milk or oat milk
- **1** tablespoon marshmallow syrup or fluff
- **1** teaspoon vanilla extract
- **1** cup ice
- Optional: mini marshmallows or cereal puffs for garnish

How to Make:

Blend milk, syrup, vanilla, and ice until smooth. Pour into a cup and top with mini marshmallows or crushed cereal bits.

Fun Variation: Toast a marshmallow and perch it on the rim for a s'mores-style flair.

66: Licorice Twist Slushie

Bold and unusual, this slushie draws inspiration from red licorice and candy ropes, blending a cherry base with a hint of spice.

You'll Need:

- ¾ cup cherry juice or red fruit punch
- 1 tablespoon black cherry or cinnamon syrup
- 1 cup crushed ice
- Optional: red licorice straw

How to Make:

Blend juice, syrup, and ice. Pour and serve with a red licorice stick as a fun edible straw.

Taste Tip: Add a dash of anise or cinnamon for a deeper licorice note, if you enjoy stronger flavors.

67: Chocolate-Covered Grape Slushie

This fun twist takes the idea of chocolate-dipped fruit and turns it into a frozen, grape-filled treat.

You'll Need:

- 1 cup frozen grapes
- ½ cup white grape juice
- 1 tablespoon chocolate syrup
- 1 cup crushed ice
- Optional: cocoa nibs or chocolate chips on top

How to Make:

Blend grapes, juice, syrup, and ice until smooth. Pour and top with cocoa nibs or a drizzle of extra syrup.

Creative Option: Swirl in a spoonful of yogurt for a creamy effect that mimics chocolate fondue.

68: Sweet Tart Slushie

Bright, tangy, and a little puckery—just like a roll of Sweet Tarts. This slushie balances fruity flavors with a lemony twist.

You'll Need:

- ½ cup lemonade
- ¼ cup cranberry juice
- ¼ cup orange juice
- 1 teaspoon lime juice
- 1 tablespoon honey (optional)
- 1½ cups crushed ice

How to Make:

Blend all ingredients until slushy and frothy. Taste and add honey if it's too tart for your liking.

Color Tip: Use frozen fruit instead of ice for a deeper, richer tone—frozen cherries, raspberries, or oranges work well here.

69: Caramel Apple Slushie

This fall-favorite candy flavor turns into a chilled treat that's part tart, part sweet, and totally delicious.

You'll Need:

- ¾ cup apple juice or cider
- ½ cup crushed green apple slices (frozen if possible)
- 1 tablespoon caramel syrup
- 1 cup crushed ice
- Optional: drizzle of extra caramel on top

How to Make:

Blend apple juice, frozen apples, caramel syrup, and ice until thick. Pour into a glass and swirl with more caramel.

Fun Option: Serve with a thin apple wedge on the rim and a cinnamon stick stirrer.

70: Chocolate-Mint Patty Slushie

Inspired by chocolate mint patties, this slushie is refreshing and rich—a great after-dinner frozen drink.

You'll Need:

- ¾ cup milk or chocolate milk
- **1** tablespoon cocoa powder or chocolate syrup
- ½ teaspoon peppermint extract
- **1** cup crushed ice
- Optional: crushed chocolate mints or whipped cream

How to Make:

Blend milk, chocolate, peppermint, and ice until smooth. Pour and top with crushed mint candies or whipped cream.

Cool Tip: Use mint chocolate chip ice cream instead of cocoa and milk for a dessert-style version.

Wrap-Up: Candy Slushie Party Ideas

Now that you've got **15** candy-inspired slushie recipes, why not create a full-on frozen candy bar for your next gathering?

Candy Slushie Bar Checklist:

- **3–4** syrup flavors (cotton candy, blue raspberry, cherry, bubblegum)
- Ice, frozen fruit, and a blender
- Mini marshmallows, sour strips, rock candy, sprinkles
- Paper umbrellas, striped straws, and whipped cream
- Candy-inspired name tags: "Sour Shock," "Bubblegum Blast," "Rockin' Raspberry"

Let guests pick a base, a mix-in, and a topping. Add some fun signs, and it becomes a frozen dessert station like no other!

PART 7: Dessert-Style Smoothie Recipes

71: Strawberry Shortcake Smoothie

A creamy, fruity smoothie that tastes just like a slice of strawberry shortcake—without the baking.

You'll Need:

- ½ cup frozen strawberries
- ½ banana
- ½ cup vanilla yogurt
- ½ cup milk or almond milk
- **1** graham cracker (crushed)
- Ice

How to Make It:

1. Blend strawberries, banana, yogurt, and milk.
2. Add crushed graham cracker and ice, then blend again.
3. Pour into a chilled glass.

Sweet Twist: Top with a dollop of whipped cream and a sprinkle of graham cracker crumbs.

This smoothie is smooth, fruity, and tastes like dessert in a glass—perfect for satisfying your sweet tooth without turning on the oven.

72: Cinnamon Roll Smoothie

Rich and creamy with a warm cinnamon swirl, this smoothie captures the gooey goodness of a fresh cinnamon roll.

You'll Need:

- ½ frozen banana
- ½ cup vanilla yogurt
- ¾ cup milk or oat milk
- **1** tablespoon maple syrup
- ½ teaspoon ground cinnamon
- Ice

How to Make It:

1. Blend banana, yogurt, milk, syrup, cinnamon, and ice until thick and creamy.
2. Pour into a tall glass.

Baking Bonus: Sprinkle the top with a dash of cinnamon sugar or crushed pecans.

This smoothie is warm-spiced, indulgent, and perfect for cozy mornings or midday comfort.

73: Chocolate Peanut Butter Cup Smoothie

Just like your favorite candy cup—but blended into a smooth, cold treat that hits every craving.

You'll Need:

- **1** frozen banana
- **1** tablespoon cocoa powder or chocolate syrup
- **1** tablespoon peanut butter
- ½ cup milk
- ½ cup Greek yogurt
- Ice

How to Make It:

1. Blend all ingredients until rich and creamy.
2. Add more milk for a thinner drink, or more ice for thicker texture.
3. Pour and serve with shaved chocolate or peanut pieces.

Optional Add-In: A small scoop of protein powder for extra fuel.

It's sweet, salty, chocolatey, and incredibly satisfying.

74: Banana Cream Pie Smoothie

Creamy, mellow, and naturally sweet—this smoothie tastes like banana pie filling, straight from the blender.

You'll Need:

- **1** ripe banana
- ½ cup vanilla yogurt or banana-flavored yogurt
- ¾ cup milk
- ½ teaspoon vanilla extract
- **1** graham cracker (optional)
- Ice

How to Make It:

1. Blend banana, yogurt, milk, and vanilla until smooth.

2. Add graham cracker and ice, and blend again.

3. Serve in a mason jar with a banana slice on top.

Dessert Trick: Top with whipped cream for full pie effect.

This one's a hit with kids and grownups, especially when you want something creamy but refreshing.

75: Key Lime Pie Smoothie

Tart, creamy, and just sweet enough, this smoothie captures the flavor of classic key lime pie.

You'll Need:

- Juice of **2** limes
- ½ frozen banana
- ½ cup vanilla yogurt
- ½ cup coconut milk or regular milk
- **1** graham cracker (crushed)
- **1** teaspoon honey (optional)
- Ice

How to Make It:

1. Blend lime juice, banana, yogurt, milk, and honey.

2. Add crushed graham cracker and ice, then blend again.

3. Serve in a cold glass with a lime wedge.

Extra Zing: Add lime zest or a few drops of vanilla extract for more pie flavor.

It's tropical, tart, and a frozen vacation in a cup.

76: Cookies and Cream Smoothie

A milkshake-style smoothie made with chocolate sandwich cookies and creamy yogurt—it's a cookies-and-milk classic in drink form.

You'll Need:

- ½ cup milk
- ½ cup vanilla yogurt
- **4–5** chocolate sandwich cookies (like Oreos)
- **1** frozen banana (optional for thickness)
- Ice

How to Make It:

1. Blend milk, yogurt, and cookies.

2. Add banana and ice, then blend again until thick.

3. Serve with a cookie on the rim or crushed crumbs on top.

Fun Tip: Freeze some crushed cookies in ice cubes for a stronger flavor.

Rich, sweet, and a little crunchy—this smoothie feels like a milkshake but drinks like a snack.

77: Chocolate-Covered Cherry Smoothie

A grown-up dessert smoothie with dark cherry flavor and a chocolate swirl.

You'll Need:

- ½ cup frozen dark cherries
- **1** frozen banana
- **1** tablespoon cocoa powder or chocolate syrup
- ½ cup milk or almond milk
- ½ cup vanilla yogurt

• Ice

How to Make It:

1. Blend cherries, banana, yogurt, milk, and chocolate until smooth.

2. Pour into a glass and top with a cherry and chocolate drizzle.

Flavor Upgrade: Use almond extract for that chocolate-cherry cordial taste.

It's rich and elegant—a perfect frozen dessert for date nights or indulgent afternoons.

78: Apple Pie Smoothie

This smoothie tastes like a fresh-baked apple pie—without the crust or oven. It's warm-spiced, naturally sweet, and oh-so-satisfying.

You'll Need:

• **1** apple (peeled and chopped, or ½ cup unsweetened applesauce)

• ½ frozen banana

• ½ cup vanilla yogurt

• ¾ cup milk or almond milk

• ½ teaspoon cinnamon

• **1** graham cracker (optional)

• Ice

How to Make It:

1. Blend apple, banana, yogurt, milk, and cinnamon.

2. Add ice and graham cracker, then blend again.

3. Serve in a mason jar and sprinkle with a dash of cinnamon.

Cozy Twist: Add a touch of nutmeg or maple syrup to enhance the pie flavor.

It's comfort in a cup—perfect for chilly mornings or dessert-style snacking.

79: Chocolate Banana Split Smoothie

Inspired by the classic banana split, this smoothie is chocolatey, creamy, and topped with your favorite sundae garnishes.

You'll Need:

• **1** banana

• **1** tablespoon chocolate syrup

• ½ cup vanilla yogurt

• ½ cup milk

• **1** tablespoon peanut butter (optional)

• Ice

How to Make It:

1. Blend banana, yogurt, chocolate syrup, and milk.

2. Add peanut butter and ice, then blend again.

3. Pour into a sundae glass.

Sundae Style: Top with whipped cream, rainbow sprinkles, and a maraschino cherry.

This smoothie is rich, playful, and perfect when you're craving dessert for breakfast.

80: Blueberry Cheesecake Smoothie

A smoothie with the tang of cream cheese and the sweetness of blueberries—it's like sipping a slice of cheesecake.

You'll Need:

• ½ cup frozen blueberries

• ¼ banana

• **2** tablespoons cream cheese

• ½ cup milk

• ½ cup vanilla yogurt

• **1** graham cracker (crushed)

• Ice

How to Make It:

1. Blend blueberries, banana, cream cheese, yogurt, and milk.

2. Add crushed graham cracker and ice. Blend until thick.

3. Pour and garnish with extra berries or a swirl of whipped topping.

Dessert Bonus: Freeze leftovers into mini cheesecake smoothie pops.

This is a creamy and elegant dessert drink with just the right amount of fruity tartness.

81: Pumpkin Pie Smoothie

This fall favorite brings pumpkin, spice, and everything nice into one creamy glass.

You'll Need:

- ½ cup canned pumpkin puree
- ½ frozen banana
- ½ cup vanilla yogurt
- ¾ cup milk or oat milk
- ½ teaspoon pumpkin pie spice
- **1** graham cracker (optional)
- Ice

How to Make It:

1. Blend pumpkin, banana, yogurt, milk, and spice.

2. Add crushed graham cracker and ice, then blend again.

3. Serve with a sprinkle of cinnamon or nutmeg on top.

Flavor Tip: Add a splash of maple syrup for added warmth.

It's a comforting, seasonal smoothie perfect for cozy mornings or holiday dessert swaps.

82: Chocolate Chip Cookie Dough Smoothie

A fun treat that tastes like sneaking a spoonful of cookie dough—only frozen and blended.

You'll Need:

- ½ frozen banana
- ½ cup vanilla yogurt
- **1** tablespoon peanut butter or almond butter
- **1** tablespoon mini chocolate chips
- **1** teaspoon vanilla extract
- ½ cup milk
- Ice

How to Make It:

1. Blend banana, yogurt, peanut butter, vanilla, and milk.

2. Add chocolate chips and ice. Pulse briefly to keep texture.

3. Pour and top with extra chips or cookie crumbs.

Texture Tip: Blend longer for a smooth shake, or pulse to keep little cookie bits.

This is an after-school snack or late-night dessert in drinkable form.

83: Carrot Cake Smoothie

Sweet and spiced like a slice of carrot cake—this smoothie adds veggies in a delicious way.

You'll Need:

- ½ cup finely grated carrot (or use pre-steamed carrots)
- ½ frozen banana
- ½ cup vanilla Greek yogurt
- ¾ cup milk or almond milk
- ½ teaspoon cinnamon
- ⅛ teaspoon nutmeg

- **1** tablespoon raisins (optional)
- Ice

How to Make It:

1. Blend carrot, banana, yogurt, milk, and spices until smooth.

2. Add raisins and ice, then blend again.

3. Top with chopped walnuts or a swirl of yogurt.

Sneaky Veggie Win: Add a few chunks of pineapple or apple for natural sweetness.

This smoothie is healthy, creative, and surprisingly indulgent.

84: Mocha Fudge Smoothie

Rich, chocolatey, and lightly caffeinated, this smoothie tastes like a frozen mocha milkshake.

You'll Need:

- ½ cup cold brew coffee or strong chilled coffee
- ½ frozen banana
- **1** tablespoon cocoa powder
- ½ cup milk or oat milk
- **1** tablespoon maple syrup or chocolate syrup
- ½ cup vanilla yogurt
- Ice

How to Make It:

1. Blend coffee, banana, cocoa, yogurt, and milk.

2. Add syrup and ice. Blend until creamy and thick.

3. Pour and top with whipped cream and a dusting of cocoa powder.

Energy Tip: Add a scoop of protein powder or flaxseed to make it a power drink.

This is a perfect smoothie for mornings, afternoon pick-me-ups, or dessert with a buzz.

PART 8: Seasonal & Holiday Slushies

85: Winter Wonderland Peppermint Slushie

This chilly treat captures the spirit of winter with a frosty peppermint twist. It's icy, refreshing, and perfect for holiday parties.

You'll Need:

- ¾ cup milk or almond milk
- ½ teaspoon peppermint extract
- **1** tablespoon white chocolate syrup or vanilla syrup
- **1** cup crushed ice
- Optional: crushed peppermint candies and whipped cream

How to Make It:

1. Blend milk, peppermint extract, syrup, and ice until smooth.

2. Pour into a frosted glass.

3. Top with whipped cream and crushed candy for a snow-like effect.

Holiday Tip: Add a mini candy cane on the rim or serve with a red-and-white striped straw.

This slushie brings holiday cheer in every sip—cool, creamy, and peppermint-perfect.

86: Spring Berry Bloom Slushie

Celebrate springtime with this vibrant mix of berries, floral notes, and a splash of citrus.

You'll Need:

- ½ cup frozen strawberries
- ½ cup frozen raspberries
- Juice of **1** lemon
- **1** tablespoon honey or agave
- ¾ cup cold water or berry tea
- Ice

How to Make It:

1. Blend berries, lemon juice, sweetener, and tea with ice.

2. Pour into a clear glass and garnish with an edible flower or fresh mint.

Floral Twist: Add a few drops of rose water or lavender syrup for a garden-fresh vibe.

This slushie is light, fruity, and bursting with spring flavors—perfect for brunches or outdoor gatherings.

87: Firecracker Cherry Lime Slushie (4th of July)

A bright red-and-green frozen drink that's bold, tangy, and fun for Independence Day or any summer festivity.

You'll Need:

- ½ cup cherry juice
- Juice of **1** lime
- **1** tablespoon cherry syrup
- **1** cup crushed ice
- Optional: blue raspberry syrup or blueberries for color contrast

How to Make It:

1. Blend cherry juice, lime juice, syrup, and ice.

2. Pour and garnish with a lime wedge or a firecracker straw.

3. Optional: layer with blue raspberry slushie for a red-white-blue effect.

Party Tip: Freeze into cups the night before and stir before serving for a no-blender needed treat.

It's tart, sweet, and packed with summer energy.

88: Autumn Spiced Apple Slushie

This cozy-meets-cold drink is a chilled version of warm apple cider, perfect for early fall afternoons.

You'll Need:

- ¾ cup apple cider
- ½ frozen apple (or ½ cup applesauce)
- ¼ teaspoon cinnamon
- Pinch of nutmeg
- **1** cup crushed ice
- Optional: caramel drizzle

How to Make It:

1. Blend cider, apple, spices, and ice until slushy.
2. Drizzle caramel on the inside of the glass before pouring.
3. Garnish with a cinnamon stick or apple slice.

Fall Favorite: Add a dash of clove or ginger for extra spice.

It's the taste of autumn in a frosty glass—warm-flavored but ice-cold.

89: Summer Sunset Slushie

A tropical blend inspired by warm nights and golden skies, this drink layers mango and pineapple with a splash of citrus.

You'll Need:

- ½ cup frozen mango chunks
- ½ cup frozen pineapple
- ¾ cup orange juice
- **1** tablespoon lime juice
- **1** cup crushed ice

How to Make It:

1. Blend mango, pineapple, juice, and lime until thick and icy.
2. Pour into a tall glass and garnish with a pineapple wedge.

Layer Tip: Reserve some orange juice and layer it separately for a two-tone sunset effect.

This slushie is refreshing, tangy, and beach-day ready.

90: Halloween Candy Corn Slushie

Inspired by the colors (not the taste) of candy corn, this slushie layers mango, pineapple, and coconut for a creamy fall treat.

You'll Need:

Yellow layer: ½ cup mango + ½ cup orange juice

Orange layer: ½ cup pineapple + ½ banana + ¼ cup milk

White layer: ½ cup coconut milk + ¼ cup vanilla yogurt

- Crushed ice as needed

How to Make It:

1. Blend each layer separately with ice.
2. Freeze each for **10** minutes between pours to keep colors distinct.
3. Assemble: yellow on bottom, orange in middle, white on top.

Spooky Flair: Add candy eyes or sprinkles on top.

It's a fun Halloween slushie that's more fruity than sugary, but still festive and fun.

91: Valentine's Strawberry Rose Slushie

Romantic and sweet, this pink drink pairs strawberry with delicate rose flavor for a classy twist.

You'll Need:

- **1** cup frozen strawberries
- ¾ cup coconut milk or almond milk
- **1** teaspoon rose water
- **1** tablespoon honey or maple syrup
- Ice

How to Make It:

1. Blend strawberries, milk, rose water, and sweetener with ice.

2. Pour into a fancy glass and top with edible rose petals or a chocolate heart.

Romantic Tip: Add a splash of vanilla for a creamy finish.

It's perfect for Valentine's Day, anniversaries, or when you want something elegant and special.

PART 9: Protein & Energy Smoothie Recipes

92: Classic Peanut Butter Banana Power Smoothie

This smoothie blends protein, potassium, and creaminess for a satisfying and energizing boost.

You'll Need:

- **1** frozen banana
- **1** tablespoon peanut butter
- **1** scoop vanilla or chocolate protein powder
- ½ cup Greek yogurt
- ¾ cup milk or oat milk
- Ice

How to Make It:

1. Blend all ingredients until smooth and thick.
2. Add more milk for a thinner texture.
3. Pour and sprinkle crushed peanuts or granola on top.

Power Tip: Add a dash of cinnamon or flaxseed for extra nutrients.

This smoothie is perfect for mornings, workouts, or a filling afternoon snack.

93: Chocolate Almond Energy Smoothie

Nutty, rich, and full of healthy fats and protein, this smoothie tastes like dessert while fueling your body.

You'll Need:

- **1** tablespoon almond butter
- **1** scoop chocolate protein powder
- **1** frozen banana
- ¾ cup almond milk
- **1** tablespoon cocoa powder
- Ice

How to Make It:

1. Blend almond butter, protein, banana, milk, cocoa, and ice.
2. Blend until creamy and pour into a chilled cup.

Upgrade Tip: Top with sliced almonds or dark chocolate shavings.

This drink is indulgent and energizing, ideal for powering through long days.

94: Berry Oat Breakfast Smoothie

This smoothie combines antioxidants, fiber, and slow-digesting oats for a hearty, wake-up blend.

You'll Need:

- ½ cup frozen mixed berries
- ¼ cup quick oats
- ½ cup Greek yogurt
- ¾ cup milk or water
- **1** teaspoon honey (optional)
- Ice

How to Make It:

1. Blend all ingredients together until smooth.
2. Let sit for **2** minutes so the oats thicken.
3. Serve with a sprinkle of granola on top.

Hearty Variation: Add a spoonful of nut butter or chia seeds.

This smoothie is perfect for busy mornings or breakfast on the go.

95: Tropical Protein Refresher

A light, fruity blend with coconut and pineapple flavors, this smoothie is refreshing and protein-rich without feeling heavy.

You'll Need:

- ½ cup frozen pineapple
- ½ frozen banana
- **1** scoop unflavored or vanilla protein powder
- ½ cup coconut water
- ½ cup almond or oat milk
- Ice

How to Make It:

1. Blend pineapple, banana, protein, liquids, and ice until frothy.
2. Pour and garnish with shredded coconut or a pineapple wedge.

Post-Workout Twist: Add a pinch of sea salt for hydration recovery.

This smoothie hydrates and refuels without weighing you down.

96: Green Protein Power Smoothie

A veggie-rich, energizing smoothie with a touch of fruit and protein for a clean, nutrient-packed option.

You'll Need:

- **1** cup spinach or kale (stems removed)
- ½ frozen banana
- ½ apple or ½ cup pineapple
- **1** scoop vanilla protein powder
- ¾ cup almond milk or water
- Ice

How to Make It:

1. Blend greens, fruit, protein, and liquid.
2. Add ice and blend again until smooth.

Green Tip: Add a squeeze of lemon or lime to brighten the flavor.

This smoothie is clean, energizing, and perfect for mornings when you need a boost.

97: Mocha Morning Fuel Smoothie

Coffee meets protein in this energizing blend that satisfies caffeine cravings and hunger at once.

You'll Need:

- ½ cup cold brew coffee or chilled espresso
- ½ frozen banana
- **1** scoop chocolate or mocha protein powder
- ¼ cup Greek yogurt
- ½ cup milk
- Ice

How to Make It:

1. Blend all ingredients until frothy.
2. Pour into a tall glass and sprinkle with cocoa powder.

Fuel Tip: Add oats or flaxseed for longer-lasting energy.

This smoothie is great for breakfast or an afternoon pick-me-up with lasting fuel.

98: Blueberry Chia Recovery Smoothie

Packed with antioxidants, omega-**3**s, and protein, this smoothie is great for post-exercise recovery or a clean daily snack.

You'll Need:

- ½ cup frozen blueberries
- **1** scoop vanilla protein powder
- **1** tablespoon chia seeds

- ½ cup almond milk
- ½ cup water or coconut water
- Ice

How to Make It:

1. Blend everything until smooth.
2. Let sit for **2–3** minutes to let chia seeds soften.
3. Serve with a few fresh berries on top.

Recovery Add-On: Add ½ teaspoon turmeric for anti-inflammatory benefits.

This smoothie supports recovery and overall wellness.

99: Cinnamon Date Smoothie with Oats

Naturally sweetened with dates, this smoothie offers a rich, caramel-like flavor with plenty of fiber and fuel.

You'll Need:

- **2–3** pitted Medjool dates
- ¼ cup oats
- ½ frozen banana
- ½ teaspoon cinnamon
- **1** scoop vanilla protein powder
- ¾ cup milk
- Ice

How to Make It:

1. Soak dates in warm water for **5** minutes if needed.
2. Blend all ingredients until smooth and creamy.
3. Pour and sprinkle with cinnamon or nutmeg.

Fiber Boost: Add a tablespoon of flax or hemp seeds.

This smoothie is comforting, filling, and naturally energizing.

100: Maple Vanilla Protein Shake

Smooth, lightly sweet, and comforting, this shake-style smoothie blends classic breakfast flavors with clean protein power.

You'll Need:

- **1** scoop vanilla protein powder
- **1** tablespoon pure maple syrup
- ½ frozen banana
- ¾ cup milk or oat milk
- ½ teaspoon vanilla extract
- **1** tablespoon rolled oats (optional)
- Ice

How to Make It:

1. Blend all ingredients until thick and creamy.
2. Adjust sweetness with extra maple if desired.
3. Serve with a pinch of cinnamon or a drizzle of syrup on top.

Warming Option: Skip the ice and gently warm the milk first for a cozy, drinkable "hot smoothie."

This shake is great for those who prefer mellow flavors—smooth, nourishing, and just sweet enough to start your day right.

PART 10: Copycat Slushie Recipes

101: Cherry Limeade Slushie (Inspired by Sonic)

This sweet-and-tangy favorite is the ultimate drive-thru treat—now easy to blend at home.

You'll Need:

- ½ cup lemon-lime soda
- ¼ cup cherry juice
- Juice of ½ lime
- **1** tablespoon grenadine or cherry syrup
- **1** cup crushed ice
- Optional: maraschino cherry and lime slice for garnish

How to Make It:

1. Blend soda, cherry juice, lime juice, syrup, and ice until slushy.
2. Pour into a tall glass.
3. Top with a cherry and lime slice.

Extra Fizz Tip: Stir in extra soda after blending for more bubbles.

It's fruity, fizzy, and fun—just like your favorite takeout order.

102: Frozen Coca-Cola Slushie

Recreate the movie-theater or amusement park classic with just a bottle of soda and a blender.

You'll Need:

- 1½ cups Coca-Cola (or any cola)
- 1½ cups crushed ice
- Optional: a splash of cherry syrup or vanilla extract

How to Make It:

1. Pour soda into the blender and let it sit **1–2** minutes to reduce fizz.
2. Add ice and optional flavoring.
3. Blend quickly until slushy and pour immediately.

Flavor Add-On: Try it with frozen cola cubes instead of regular ice for a stronger taste.

This one's simple but unbeatable when you want a nostalgic, ice-cold cola fix.

103: Blue Raspberry Icee Slushie

Channel that classic gas station slushie flavor with this bright and bold blend.

You'll Need:

- ¾ cup lemon-lime soda
- **2** tablespoons blue raspberry syrup
- **1** cup crushed ice
- Optional: a pinch of citric acid or lemon juice for tartness

How to Make It:

1. Blend soda, syrup, and ice until smooth.
2. Add citric acid or lemon for extra zing.
3. Serve in a clear cup with a striped straw.

Colorful Tip: Layer with a cherry slushie for a red-and-blue ICEE combo.

It's tangy, sweet, and totally reminiscent of summer convenience store stops.

104: Mango Dragonfruit Slush (Inspired by Starbucks Refresher)

This tropical blend is just like the colorful favorite—but made without a long line or high price.

You'll Need:

- ½ cup mango juice
- ¼ cup white grape juice
- **2** tablespoons freeze-dried dragonfruit (or use frozen cubes)
- **1** cup ice
- Optional: coconut milk for a creamier version

How to Make It:

1. Blend juices, dragonfruit, and ice until smooth.

2. For a creamy version, add a splash of coconut milk and blend again.

3. Pour and enjoy that vivid pink color!

Barista Hack: Add green tea or a caffeine shot for extra energy.

It's vibrant, fruity, and perfect for refreshment on sunny days.

105: Tropical Slushie (Inspired by Taco Bell Freeze)

Bright, citrusy, and perfect for taco night, this frozen drink mimics Taco Bell's rotating Freeze flavors.

You'll Need:

- ½ cup orange juice
- ¼ cup pineapple juice
- **1** tablespoon lime juice
- **1** tablespoon mango or passionfruit syrup
- **1**½ cups crushed ice

How to Make It:

1. Blend juices, syrup, and ice until thick and icy.

2. Serve with a wedge of lime or a straw in a taco-themed cup.

Menu Match: Try layering two flavors for a frozen "swirl" like their dual Freeze options.

It's fast food fun—without the drive-thru.

106: Frozen Lemonade Slushie (Inspired by Chick-fil-A)

This creamy-meets-tart frozen lemonade is a perfect summer drink, now in slushie form.

You'll Need:

- ¾ cup fresh lemonade
- ¼ cup vanilla soft-serve or Greek yogurt
- **1–1**½ cups crushed ice
- Optional: lemon zest for brightness

How to Make It:

1. Blend lemonade, soft-serve or yogurt, and ice until creamy and frosty.

2. Pour into a cup and garnish with lemon zest or a lemon wheel.

Creamy Tip: Add a splash of sweetened condensed milk for extra indulgence.

This drink is tangy, smooth, and perfectly refreshing on hot days.

107: Carnival Orange Cream Slushie (Inspired by Orange Julius)

This orange-vanilla slushie is sweet, smooth, and a retro favorite from mall food courts and fairgrounds.

You'll Need:

- ½ cup orange juice
- ¼ cup milk or almond milk
- ¼ cup vanilla yogurt
- **1** teaspoon vanilla extract
- **1** tablespoon sugar or honey (optional)
- **1** cup crushed ice

How to Make It:

1. Blend all ingredients until thick and frothy.

2. Pour into a clear cup and serve with an orange slice.

Memory Lane Tip: Add a scoop of vanilla protein powder to turn it into a breakfast shake.

It's a creamy blast from the past—with modern flexibility.

108: Watermelon Slushie (Inspired by Jamba Juice Watermelon Breeze)

Light, juicy, and hydrating, this frozen watermelon blend is perfect for hot days and tastes just like the Jamba Juice summer favorite.

You'll Need:

- **1** cup frozen watermelon cubes
- ½ cup strawberries (fresh or frozen)
- ¾ cup coconut water or white grape juice
- **1** teaspoon lime juice
- Ice as needed

How to Make It:

1. Blend watermelon, strawberries, juice, and lime until smooth.
2. Add ice if needed for a thicker texture.
3. Pour into a tall glass and garnish with a mini watermelon wedge.

Hydration Tip: Use coconut water to make it extra refreshing post-workout.

This slushie is fruity, sweet, and incredibly thirst-quenching.

109: Frozen Matcha Slushie (Inspired by Dunkin' Green Tea Coolatta)

A chilled green tea treat with a creamy edge—this slushie balances calm energy with cool sweetness.

You'll Need:

- **1** teaspoon matcha powder
- ½ cup milk or almond milk
- ½ cup cold water
- **1** tablespoon honey or simple syrup
- **1** cup crushed ice

How to Make It:

1. Whisk matcha powder into the water until smooth.
2. Blend with milk, honey, and ice until slushy.
3. Pour into a glass and serve with a dusting of matcha or whipped cream.

Zen Upgrade: Add vanilla protein powder for a satisfying morning shake.

Cool, earthy, and energizing—this one's for green tea lovers.

110: Carnival Grape Slushie (Inspired by 7-Eleven Slurpee)

A bold, juicy grape slush that tastes like summer fairs and corner store pit stops—sweet, purple, and nostalgic.

You'll Need:

- ¾ cup grape soda
- **1** tablespoon grape syrup
- **1**½ cups crushed ice
- Optional: lemon juice for tartness

How to Make It:

1. Let soda sit for **1–2** minutes to reduce foam.
2. Blend with syrup and ice until slushy.
3. Pour into a tall cup with a dome lid and wide straw.

Throwback Trick: Serve in a paper cup with retro stickers for a real-deal Slurpee vibe.

This slushie is sweet, fizzy, and guaranteed to please grape lovers of all ages.

Would you like to move on to Part **10**: Final Tips & Make-Your-Own Slushie Templates, or add bonus pages like flavor mix charts, serving suggestions, or certificate-style recipe trackers?

Creative Techniques & Tips

CHAPTER 11: Mixing Colors & Swirls

Color is one of the most exciting parts of frozen drinks. From deep reds to bright blues, layered slushies can look just as amazing as they taste. The key is learning how to mix and swirl colors without them blending into a dull mix.

Color Layering Tips:

- **Use bold colors:** Blue raspberry, strawberry, mango, and grape create strong contrast.
- **Freeze layers in between:** Pour your first layer into a glass and freeze it for **10–15** minutes before adding the next.
- **Spoon in carefully:** When pouring new layers, use the back of a spoon to slow the pour and prevent mixing.
- **Create swirls:** Drag a spoon or straw gently through the layers after pouring to create swirl effects.

Swirl Combos to Try:

- Strawberry + Banana
- Blue Raspberry + Lemonade
- Peach + Mango + Coconut

These drinks turn into edible art, and kids especially love seeing their creations take shape.

CHAPTER 12: Matching Flavors with Snacks & Desserts

Want to take your slushies and smoothies to the next level? Match them with snacks, meals, or desserts for a perfect flavor experience.

Fruit Pairing Guide:

- Strawberry slushie + chocolate chip cookies
- Pineapple smoothie + coconut macaroons
- Citrus slushie + salty pretzels or popcorn
- Mango smoothie + spiced crackers or banana chips
- Berry smoothies + Greek yogurt parfaits

Snack Boards with Slushies:

Make a "Frozen Treat Platter" with mini slushies in small cups paired with:

- Trail mix
- Cheese cubes
- Granola bites
- Dried fruit

Themed Nights:

Try "Taco Tuesday" with a lime slushie, or a "Movie Sundae Bar" with dessert smoothies and toppings. Coordinating flavors makes the whole experience more enjoyable and memorable.

CHAPTER 13: How to Make Slushie Art with Layers

Layered slushie art is like a frozen rainbow in a cup. It's easy once you know the technique and use the right ingredients.

Layering Rules:

1. Thicker layers go first. Dense, fruit-heavy blends sink.
2. Use color order. Stack from darkest to lightest (purple > red > orange > yellow > green > blue).
3. Freeze in stages. Let each layer firm up before adding the next.
4. Choose clear cups. This shows off your art.

Example: Tropical Rainbow Slush

- Purple: grape juice + ice
- Red: strawberries + lemonade
- Orange: mango + orange juice
- Yellow: pineapple + coconut water
- Green: kiwi + lime juice
- Blue: blue raspberry syrup + water

Finishing Touches:

- Top with fruit chunks, sprinkles, or an umbrella.
- Add a matching straw for each layer's color.

Slushie art is perfect for parties, photos, or just to brighten your day.

CHAPTER 14: Pouring, Chilling, and Serving Tricks

Little details in how you pour and serve your frozen drinks can turn a regular recipe into something unforgettable.

Pouring Tips:

- Use a spouted cup or small pitcher. This gives better control.
- Angle your glass. This helps layers settle evenly and prevents bubbles.
- Use cold glasses. Chill your serving glass in the freezer for **10** minutes before pouring.

Chilling Tricks:

- Use frozen fruit instead of ice to keep drinks from watering down.
- Keep a few smoothies in freezer-safe jars and thaw for **10** minutes before serving.
- Freeze juice cubes to use instead of regular ice for long-lasting flavor.

Serving Upgrades:

- Use mason jars with handles for a rustic touch.
- Try small glass bottles for mini slushie tastings.
- Decorate the rim with sugar, crushed candy, or citrus peel.

These tricks elevate your frozen drinks while keeping them practical and fun.

CHAPTER 15: Fruit Juice Fusion Ideas

Juice fusion is the art of combining juices to create custom slushie flavors. It's fun, easy, and gives you endless combinations.

Juice Fusion Basics:

- Mix acidic juices (like orange or lemon) with sweet juices (like grape or apple).
- Add coconut water, tea, or soda for texture and fizz.
- Try blending with frozen fruit for added thickness.

Flavor Ideas:

- Berry Sunrise: cranberry + orange + strawberry
- Tropical Tango: mango + pineapple + coconut water
- Citrus Splash: grapefruit + lemonade + lime
- Melon Mix-Up: watermelon + white grape juice

How to Use:

- Blend directly with ice for a slushie
- Freeze in cubes to drop into smoothies
- Pour over shaved ice for a snow cone twist

Juice fusions are an easy way to explore new flavors without needing syrups or dairy.

CHAPTER 16: Turning Any Fruit into a Slushy

Almost any fruit can be turned into a slushie with the right method. Even fruits that aren't usually used in drinks—like apples, pears, or grapes—can become frozen treats.

Steps:

1. Wash, peel (if needed), and chop fruit into small chunks.
2. Freeze the chunks for at least **2** hours.
3. Blend with ½ to ¾ cup of juice, lemonade, or water.
4. Add crushed ice if needed for thicker texture.
5. Blend until smooth and pour immediately.

Great Slushie Fruits:

- Apple + cinnamon + lemon juice
- Pear + vanilla + grape juice
- Grapes + lime + a splash of soda
- Kiwi + pineapple + mint

Texture Tip: Some fruits (like melons) have more water, so you may not need extra liquid. Test as you go!

This chapter opens the door to experimenting with whatever fruit is in season—or in your fridge.

CHAPTER 17: Creative Uses for Leftover Smoothies

Got a little smoothie left in the blender? Don't waste it. There are so many fun and practical ways to use your leftovers.

1. Smoothie Popsicles

- Pour leftovers into ice pop molds and freeze.
- Add a fruit slice to the mold before freezing for decoration.

2. Ice Cubes for Later

- Freeze in trays and use in tomorrow's drink for flavor and chill.
- Drop them into water, lemonade, or soda for added fun.

3. Mini Smoothie Bowls

- Pour into a small bowl and top with chopped fruit and granola.
- Add chia seeds or nut butter for a mini snack.

4. Pancake Topping

- Warm up berry smoothie leftovers for a fruity syrup.
- Pour over pancakes or waffles for a fruity twist.

This makes smoothie-making feel even more rewarding—and creative!

CHAPTER 18: Chill & Store – Keeping Slushies Fresh

While slushies are best enjoyed right after blending, there are smart ways to prep ahead or save what you don't finish.

Short-Term Storage (1–2 Hours):

- Keep your slushie in the freezer in an insulated cup or thermos.
- Stir every **30** minutes to keep the texture smooth.

Overnight Storage:

- Store in freezer-safe jars or containers with lids.
- To serve, let thaw for **10–15** minutes, stir, and enjoy.

Batch Prep Tips:

- Pre-portion fruit and juice in freezer bags.
- Label each with the flavor combo so you can grab and blend.

Don't Store With Dairy:

Smoothies made with milk or yogurt change texture if frozen too long. Use dairy-free bases or serve those fresh.

With these storage tips, your frozen treats can be ready whenever you need a quick sip or surprise guest refreshment.

CHAPTER 19: Using Sherbet and Sorbet in Frozen Drinks

Sherbet and sorbet add vibrant flavor, bold color, and creamy texture to frozen drinks—without the need for dairy or added syrups.

You'll Need:

- **1–2** scoops of your favorite sherbet or sorbet (orange, raspberry, lemon, mango)
- ¾ cup soda, lemonade, or fruit juice
- **1** cup crushed ice

How to Make It:

1. Add sherbet or sorbet to your blender along with ice and liquid.
2. Blend until thick, smooth, and fluffy.
3. Serve in a tall cup with a spoon or thick straw.

Flavor Ideas:

- Orange sherbet + lemon-lime soda = Creamsicle Slushie
- Raspberry sorbet + lemonade = Berry Blush Freeze
- Mango sorbet + pineapple juice = Tropical Sunset Chill

Tip: Sorbet is dairy-free and more fruit-forward, while sherbet has a small amount of milk for creaminess.

These ingredients elevate texture and cut down on added sweeteners, making drinks smoother and more flavorful.

CHAPTER 20: Ninja Blender Hacks for Maximum Chill

The Ninja blender is powerful and versatile—perfect for crushing ice and making flawless slushies. A few clever tricks can make it even better.

Best Practices:

- Add liquids first: Always pour your base (juice, soda, milk) in before solid ingredients to avoid jamming.
- Use crushed or small ice cubes: These blend faster and reduce stress on the blades.
- Pulse before blending: A few quick pulses help break down big chunks before full blending.

Chill-Boosting Hacks:

- Freeze your blender jar: Pop the jar in the freezer for **5–10** minutes before blending for extra frostiness.
- Pre-freeze fruit: Cut and freeze ripe fruit in small bags for ready-to-blend ingredients that act like ice.
- Use frozen juice cubes: Freeze fruit juice or tea in ice trays to keep flavor strong without watering down your drink.

Cleanup Hack:

Fill halfway with warm water and a drop of dish soap, then pulse to self-clean.

These tips help you get colder, creamier slushies every time—with no chunks and no frustration.